COMMON GROUND FOR US

ALSO BY CARL NORDGREN

Nonfiction:

Becoming a Creative Genious {Again}

Fiction:

The 53rd Parallel

Worlds Between

Anung's Journey

Common Ground for US

WARNING! THIS BOOK MAKES FOLKS OPTIMISTIC

CARL NORDGREN

Vista, CA

ISBN: 978-1-61153-628-7 (paperback)

ISBN: 978-1-61153-629-4 (ebook)

ISBN: 978-1-61153-630-0 (large print)

Library of Congress Control Number: 2026909724

Common Ground for US is published by: Torchflame Books, an imprint of Top Reads Publishing, LLC, 1035 E. Vista Way, Suite 205, Vista, CA 92084, USA

Cover design and interior layout: Jori Hanna

All of my life's work is dedicated to my wife, Marie.
The moment I saw her I knew we'd get married.
Later this year we'll celebrate our 46th anniversary.

I want to thank all my Duke students who taught me the best ways to share these ideas about becoming our most creative and entrepreneurial selves. And it's a long list of friends and colleagues who have shared insights and stories with me that have shaped this book.

CONTENTS

PREFACE

Common Ground for US was near the end of the publisher's editing process when a US Senate committee released their report predicting, and warning, that 90 million of our country's 160 million jobs could be eliminated in the next ten years as businesses replace employees with AI and robotics.

You'll find the book is shaped by the idea that no one can predict what will happen as we face a future of unknowable unknowns, so I don't believe this prediction is accurate.

I do believe it is indicative.

The book shows how each of us can best prepare to successfully make our way in an unknowable future and offers communications strategies and policy ideas for politicians and community leaders to help them create advantages for all of us.

LET'S START RIGHT HERE, RIGHT NOW

FIRST AND FOREMOST, I LOVE YOU. I LOVE YOU AND your family and friends and their family and friends' family, and I hope you feel that love on every page. I've had a large capacity for loving most of my life, and it's wonderful. With this book completed, I'm looking for more ways to be of service to you and yours.

Yes, ideas in the book are introduced and revisited, and in some cases, many times. Is this unnecessary redundancy? No, it's informed by the realization and experience of a former CEO; folks understand an idea is important to the company when it's repeated. And it's my understanding and experience as a teacher that when I repeat a topic later, it's quite likely folks will be thinking differently when it next comes around, expanding and deepening the understanding they're creating.

And now, do you know how a caterpillar becomes a butterfly?

I've spent lots of time in woods and fields and creeks, and as a kid, it didn't take long to figure out the process behind a tadpole becoming a frog. I watched dozens of times as some part of what it was could still be seen in what it was becoming, and what it was becoming retained characteristics of what it had been.

But I could never get a handle on how a caterpillar becomes a butterfly; no element of butterfly design called on any element of caterpillar design.

Then I read how it happens; it's so cool that I need to share it with you right away, so let's call on the monarch to teach us.

The monarch spends ten to fourteen days as a black-white-yellow-green striped crawling caterpillar. It sheds its skin four or five times as it grows; with the last shedding, the skin splits, revealing the bright-green chrysalis forming within.

Inside this case, the caterpillar is digesting itself, becoming a chaotic ooze except for the few cells that maintain structural integrity. These cells locate and move towards each other—the ooze is defensive, the cells struggle—and when clustered in a critical mass, they vibrate at the same frequency. These cells are pluripotent, capable of dividing into a range of cell and tissue types, and they do.

And then the glorious monarch emerges, to live as a butterfly for at least twice as long as it did as a caterpillar, unless it's of the last hatch, whose migratory offspring live up to nine months.

The scientist who studied this phenomenon named those few cells that carry the code and directions for taking on the chaos and crafting a butterfly from it "imaginal cells"—and I'll bet that name excites you. When I read it, I decided to be an imaginal cell.

Since our early history, our nation has been a caterpillar, efficiently effective at moving straight ahead and consuming all in our path. Now, was it forty years ago, it's been at least ten, that we entered the chaotic stage we are in now, where right is wrong and wrong is right, and where we are so confused we angrily consume our own foundations?

I wrote this book to share the codes and directions I've curated and collected. And it's written to support a "from now on" search for other imaginal cells, looking to achieve a critical mass to sync frequencies and help this nation emerge and flourish as the most wondrous version of itself, sustaining abundant life for centuries. My bet is you are nodding your head in agreement, that it's easy to see yourself as an imaginal cell with talents and experiences our country needs, our friends and families need, so let's get to it.

THE SOURCES OF THE BOOK'S IDEAS

THE STORY OF MY INADVERTENT DISCOVERY OF Common Ground for US provides useful perspectives on the nature of this discovery. And since its nature, you'll soon see, provides rational support for our optimistic belief that together we can flourish in face of an unknowable future, the best way to serve you is if I provide many perspectives on this all-important discovery.

It's necessary that you shape your own understandings of what Common Ground for US can mean.

The story of where it began and how it emerged is one of those perspectives you'll find useful constructing your views.

'Twas the week before Christmas 2001. A representative from Duke University's Markets and Management Studies program asked if I would teach their spring term 2002 course in Entrepreneurship to twenty-four seniors, starting in three weeks. I sang out "yes," emphatically.

I never imagined teaching a college course, but my immediate excitement about taking it on didn't surprise me. Early in my new venture days, I discovered how much I loved helping folks who'd joined us to develop their talents; it became a favorite role, CEO as servant teacher.

Later, I had the chance to guide first-time entrepreneurs, and I loved helping them learn from my successes, much more from my failures—makes sense, since I did too—and challenging them to think about, for instance, the difference between "creating advantage" versus "taking advantage" strategies for developing an opportunity, building value, and shaping organizational vibes.

The last week before we started it struck me that I had no notion of what went on inside a college classroom; what did one even look like? It had been thirty years since I was in one, and I had attended class so infrequently as a student, I had little memory of it. But I had lots of experience bringing folks together at the beginning of a new initiative, helping individuals become a team, offering open-ended invitations to move forward together toward an interesting and worthwhile goal we'd all shape along the way.

So I prepared to bring together not students, but first-time entrepreneurs. After a quick personal introduction, I said something like:

"Your turn. Who wants to talk about your venture, who you serve, the company's story?"

No hands were raised. It didn't appear as shyness.

"Okay, sure, you're Duke seniors, you're too busy to start something. Let's talk about the venture you'll be starting within five years."

No hands were raised. The obvious next question . . .

"Then why did you sign up for an entrepreneurship class if you have no interest in starting a new company?"

. . . got an immediate response, and a spirited discussion of career goals and personal aspirations soon surrounded a common theme.

The students were hoping this class would help them be more creative in their thinking, more entrepreneurial in their instincts and behaviors—not the language we used at the time, but it was what they wanted. They sensed that career success and growth—in consulting or investment banking, in business management or real estate development—would be more likely when they brought creative and entrepreneurial qualities to their work.

As their consensus grew, so did my appreciation for what they wanted; it promised to be a whole lot more fun than teaching legal and financial aspects of starting a business. Building a course to hit a target that was still being identified; that kind of challenge appealed to me.

And while I didn't fully understand it, I had a feeling that the content these students were asking for had universal importance—for entrepreneurs building new ventures and, just as important, for everyone else, for all of us, in every aspect of fully lived personal and professional lives.

What sayest thou? Is this a more useful contribution, to see myself as a creative populist committed to helping each of us and all of us become our most creative and entrepreneurial selves?

The first place I searched for content to build this course was in my work experiences; as a teenage fishing guide on the English River in the wilderness of Northwestern Ontario and the White River in the Arkansas Ozarks; as a factory and foundry worker at modest-sized regional facilities; as a copywriter and entrepreneur. In all places, in all cases, the creative behaviors needed for the jobs were abundant so the lessons to share were too.

The first two creative concepts demanding attention were story and generosity.

In 1966, as a fifteen-year-old kid guiding bank presidents

and doctors and other successful men on the English River, I discovered that when I acted on opportunities to shape the narrative of our day, I acquired more and more leadership of the day. The stories I told were the very best versions of the day my guests were living, adventurous interpretations, as flattering to the guests as I could authentically be.

Usually I was in charge by the middle of the first day; their heightened appreciation for all about them was my goal.

My understanding of the importance of generosity started strong and grew as I applied it to customers and employees throughout my start-up career. When I share the importance of being generous in business, I start with simple questions I had asked myself and my partners and folks who worked with us many times.

- Why would our customers be generous with our company unless we're generous with them?
- Why would our employees be generous with our company unless we're generous with them?
- And doesn't that sound like sustainable success, to be in generous relationships with customers and employees?

I urge folks to find out for themselves how being generous is being generative in all aspects of life by watching for generous behaviors as you go about the day and observing what happens. It's a good practice to remind ourselves to be generous in the inches and minutes of our day.

As that first semester proceeded, I stayed a step ahead, filling in the spaces the students identified and exploring other creative content sources. I started incorporating nature's lessons, wild and domestic.

The barnyard is where the difference between "climate

control" and "command and control" leadership clarifies itself; it's a challenge to get goats or chickens to do exactly what you want them to do in the moment, but fairly simple to manage the conditions around them so they want to do what you want them to do; a healthy outcome for all.

I explain to students that in a complex environment—and that's just about every system or community or ecological niche or organization you inhabit or visit—the reaction from the system to new inputs is so unpredictable you can't exercise traditional command and control leadership. You can't demand that a complex system delivers the exact output you want to achieve; the reactions from each member in the complex system incorporate their adaptations to how the other members respond and themselves adapt, making a specific output unpredictable.

Climate control leadership finds ways to influence the environment and control what you can, to make it more likely the outcomes you want to happen will happen.

More content for the class was generated by the students, who were charged to find what neuroscientists and social scientists were discovering about how, for instance, to get into your creative mind, or what creative behaviors make for effective collaboration. They prepared ten-minute presentations, including a quick overview of the research, a "back of the envelope" effort to recreate some aspect of the research, then offering practical tips supported by the research.

For example, early research concluded that the left hemisphere of your brain is the source for analytical and logical thinking, and the right hemisphere is where imagination and nonlinear thinking take place.

Now we understand that integrating your two hemispheres, so the logical is playing with the imaginative, your nonlinear and analytical thinking hold hands, is your most creative state of mind.

Research out of Stanford discovered a highly efficient and effective way to integrate your brain's hemispheres is to take a walk; integration happens just a couple of minutes after hitting your natural stride. The participants walked for thirty minutes, experiencing a 60 percent improvement in their creative idea generation.

I used to think the creative lift I enjoyed on a woods walk was from the beautifully complex, life-abundant forests and fields my dogs and I explore almost daily. The research tested walking in one of the lovely wooded parks in Palo Alto and walking on a treadmill in a basement, and it made no difference . . . it's the walking itself.

Duke scheduled me to teach their entrepreneurship course each of the next couple of semesters and the pattern repeated itself: the students were much more interested in being creative and entrepreneurial than they were in starting new ventures, so I continued to develop the course they wanted.

One improvement I made early on was adding lots of classroom exercises. You'll find some of them at the end of the Resources and Exercises section at the end of the book.

The students' benefits from this course shift were clear, I was having a blast designing and teaching it, so I approached the program's leaders, showed them what I had done to their course and why, and asked if I could develop and teach a new course titled Creativity and Entrepreneurship. They agreed.

A couple of weeks into teaching this course with "creativity" in the title, I was approached by two Duke professors who asked me something like "which academic study," or "whose definition of," "creativity" I was using for the course.

Folks, I felt foolish, as if I had been exposed as a fraud. I'd never attempted to define "creativity" and couldn't in the moment. I had spent thirty-five years living with creative people all around, I was leading a course on the topic, and it had never occurred to me that creativity needed a definition.

Back then, I couldn't define it; now I know I shouldn't.

Doesn't a definition restrict? Anything outside the chosen definition of creativity wouldn't be considered creativity, and we all need more creativity, not less, so a restrictive definition works against us.

Plus, a definition is fixed. When everything around us is continually changing, the idea that the thing we need to successfully deal with that change should have a fixed definition; doesn't it seem wrong on the face of it?

One night, driving home thinking about my inability to answer the Duke profs' challenge, I smiled at the possibility that I might be the only person to teach a course at Duke on a subject they couldn't define.

A quote from Johann Wolfgang von Goethe (1749–1832) that I love is: "Thinking is better than knowing." And while there are instances where we demand expert knowledge—the surgeon operating on your child or the engineers building a bridge—for our purposes here, Goethe's message is right on.

It is much more valuable for you to be thinking for yourself about what it means to be creative than just accepting a definition from this old dude.

Please note that "creatively entrepreneurial" will be used occasionally, and you might take a moment and wonder what that could mean to you, when those two words are linked.

I can't resist sharing this aside. Einstein believed Goethe was "the last man in the world to know everything." This is a comment about the remarkable man and about the explosive growth in knowledge since the 1800s, both in its breadth and increased specialization. And I reckon he meant the Western world, yeah?

Refusing to define creativity and urging folks to create their own multifaceted, dynamic, and situationally intelligent understanding of themselves as creative carries a responsibility. Nothing grows in a vacuum. The jazz composer and bassist Charles Mingus (1922–1979) was my guide filling the void when he said, "You can't improvise on nothing, man; you gotta improvise on something."

For years, I have collected creativity and entrepreneurial prompts, ideas and behaviors for you to riff off of, to help you craft—repeated here for emphasis—your own multifaceted, dynamic, situationally intelligent understanding of how you are and want to be creative.

You will find over seventy-five prompts in the Resources and Exercises section.

I taught at Duke for fourteen years, continually improving the class called Being Creatively Entrepreneurial. It must have been in my fourth or fifth year of teaching that I realized this love for helping each of us and all of us be our most creative selves had become a calling. I had always wanted to have a calling—my heart's delight in the service of one of the world's true needs.

Before I began teaching, I'd lived with an unexamined assumption that the human condition is creative at its core. Everywhere I worked, I was surrounded by people effectively, efficiently, often imaginatively, and usually collaboratively, getting their work done in expected and unexpected conditions.

At the foundry and on the factory floor, occasional work-arounds were needed, and the foreman or crew chief redeployed the resources they could to keep the line moving, to stay productive; it was like a backyard quarterback explaining a new play and assigning roles in the moment so Galesburg Foundry or Butler Manufacturing kept operating smoothly.

We were doing what we could with what we had where we were, a wonderfully creative strategy.

I found creativity in abundance back when I was interviewing prospective employees for ventures I helped start and grow, recruiting them to the notion that they would have two jobs if offered the opportunity to work with us.

One was the job description's job. The other was intentionally embracing the responsibility of helping the company be incredible, a place where we love to work because we trust and respect each other.

The candidates were invited to share their thoughts, questions, and experiences about this second job, and just about everyone had solid ideas for building organizational health. It didn't matter if they were accountants, technicians, graphic designers, or managers; most shared experiences that showed understanding of this challenge.

As suggested above, I never believed creativity to be the special gift of a privileged few; I saw it, I see it, as common as clay and all the more wonderful for it.

But I would never have been so bold as to declare us all creative geniuses if I hadn't learned about the research project NASA participated in; it gave me permission that I eagerly apply.

In 1962, when JFK boldly challenged NASA to send a man to walk on the moon and bring him home safely, and to complete the mission by the end of the decade, NASA and the nation responded.

Science and math were given new emphasis in public education. Astronauts' status as cultural heroes matched rock stars and home-run hitters. Schoolchildren surrounded the portable black-and-white TV a classmate had brought from home, watching flickering images of each Apollo mission's next step with anticipation and a youthful pride in our nation—my most vivid memories of being in school in those days.

Art and entertainment reflected NASA's challenge with a dramatic increase in science fiction and space travel, notably the original *Star Trek* television series, *2001: A Space Odyssey*, *Planet of the Apes*, and *Fantastic Voyage* (a trip to inner space).

The nation was excited from the start, and that excitement grew until the mid-sixties, when it faded a bit as the country's leadership shifted the focus of its storytelling. An estimated 95 percent of US citizens watched the landing, though I didn't. I was in Canada, where the only media available to me were two- or three-day-old newspapers that guests brought and left in their cabins, which would circulate through the camp.

NASA's challenge was extraordinary, cataloged in this excerpt from Kennedy's speech at Rice University's football stadium on a sunny 102-degree afternoon:

> We shall send to the moon, 240,000 miles away from the control station in Houston, a giant rocket more than 300 feet tall, the length of this football field, made of new metal alloys, some of which have not yet been invented, capable of standing heat and stresses several times more than have ever been experienced, fitted together with a precision better than the finest watch, carrying all the equipment needed for propulsion, guidance, control, communications, food and survival, on an untried mission, to an unknown celestial body, and then return it safely to earth, re-entering the atmosphere at speeds of over 25,000 miles per hour . . .

Let's keep in mind that the "equipment needed for propulsion, guidance, control, communications, food and survival" needed to be imagined, designed, and engineered as well.

NASA determined that they needed to hire the most creative, entrepreneurial, and innovative scientists and engineers they could find. They asked Dr. George Land of the University of Iowa, then considered the leading expert on assessing creativity, to develop a tool that would measure core creative cognition, intending to use it in the interview process.

When Land delivered the tool, NASA made another smart move by first assessing their current scientists and engineers, as a measure of the tool's accuracy; they were pleased with what they found. The folks delivering the breakthroughs scored by far the best, and the scores stepped down consistently with fewer innovative contributions.

It's fun to think there was a bit of scientists' whimsy when NASA called their top performers on the assessment their "creative geniuses."

A couple of years later, Dr. Land, now joined by Dr. Beth Jarman, recruited 1,600 four- and five-year-old schoolchildren to take the same assessment developed for NASA, modified for age.

When I share the results of their project at workshops or classes, I have fun wrapping it with dramatic storytelling. I remind folks that, since this was the late sixties, grading the assessments and compiling the scores was done by hand. Slowly. One at a time.

We picture a long table in a conference room, with one or two grad students who have joined Land and Jarman gathered round. The 1,600 assessments are stacked high in the middle of the table. There's late-sixties cigarette smoke drifting over the cups of coffee and half eaten sandwiches as the stacks of to-be-graded assessments shrink and the stacks of completed assessments grow . . . and so does the energy in the room, and the smiles on folks' faces, for the early scores that had seemed too good, those trends have continued, and the smiles grow larger until, finally, they finish tabulating and look at each other, delightfully stunned.

They were at the ground-zero revelation of something vitally important to each of us and all of us: 98 percent of these 1,600 four- and five-year-old children scored at NASA's creative genius level.

What? 98 percent. All of us?

Doesn't this mean every time you walk into a room, it's full of creative geniuses? For many, it's fully realized, for some it lies dormant; this quality is so fundamental to us that it doesn't go away.

Over the past couple of decades, I came to believe nothing is more important than embracing this is who we are; now I am so bold as to say nothing is as important.

At a workshop, when I reveal the finding that 98 percent of us are born with a creative genius, the room changes. There is a new energy. Folks love that this is so. They recall exploring and building as children, and they share those memories with their neighbor, enjoying being seen as the best of themselves.

Horses shake their manes excitedly when they feel the selfsame way.

After hearing this, workshop participants are ready for what comes next in ways they weren't a minute earlier. They are more confident, open, and primed to take it in and take it on, so I follow it up immediately with an exercise or game for them, acknowledging "Creative geniuses don't want to listen to me talk, they want to act, they want to imagine, they want to perform or compose or play. So for the next ten minutes . . ." And they apply their creative genius to one of the exercises in the back of this book.

So, let me ask, what would you do?

What if, after sharing this creative genius story with well over five thousand individuals—artists and software developers; entrepreneurs and scientists; military and business leaders and those who report to or work for them; lawyers and doctors and accountants; teachers and students and engineers—what if you began to suspect there's something else here, another way to shape and share this content to serve us?

When it's clear our country has the resources and the knowledge to accomplish, for instance, a sustainable abundance for all, but will continue to limp along for as long as we are so determined to be not just divided but fiercely mean about it, and you stumble upon this fertile common ground, composed of the creative qualities and attributes most valuable now and for now on, what would you do? With this insight, what will you do?

Here's what I'm doing.

After a brief glimpse of it in 2020, it was a couple of years later that I recognized that, along with being the nurturing source for teaching entrepreneurial, creative, productive, innovative, and generative energies and behaviors, this common ground 98 percent of us share has powerful potential for shaping political policy while providing productive language and behaviors for governance. And that the stories told from this common ground serve us simply in their telling.

As first ideas about this common ground's political potential found their early forms, I shared them to listen to others talk about them. What I've heard tells me you will find its value and benefits are attractive and useful to:

- the political and cultural left and right.
- our rural regions and small towns and our urban and suburban neighborhoods.
- those who have and those who don't have yet.
- folks like me, who are well into a long journey, and even more to young generations, who will live deep into this century.

There is promising agreement that our country's urgent need for unity is well served by this common ground. And there is strong accord that what I will again call "Common Ground for US' will serve each of us, our families and friends and communities, and our nation, in three important ways:

1. On this Common Ground for US, we go beyond reviving our innovative leadership; we enable and invite bottom-up self-organized creative and entrepreneurial growth; the healthiest and most sustainable.
2. On this Common Ground for US, we find the very best preparation for the unpredictable challenges and crises and the extraordinary opportunities of our unknowable future.
3. On this Common Ground for US, leaders find new ways, the best ways, to see us so they will serve us more effectively, and they will find fresh language to cultivate new perspectives on problematic political issues.

Another benefit of Common Ground for US is that no one

has claimed it, no one has shaped some understanding of it to share it with others. We arrive there together, explore its value together, continue developing its energies and ideas, and together we'll find how it helps us prepare for our future of unknowable unknowns.

I will share what my exploration has revealed, but first, the fishing guide in me wants to provide two prompts for your discovering mind.

As the ideas for this book were developing, I was reading and rereading *The Dawn of Everything*. Since the early 1900s, new archaeological evidence has led to new anthropological insights into our ancestors' social and political constructs. The authors of the book, David Graeber and David Wengrow, spent ten years studying these new findings and questioning the questions we've been asking, then spent ten years writing this great big book filled with interesting challenges to the conventional understanding of who and how we've been as we've made our way here.

And I was reading *Indigenous Continent*, by the historian Pekka Hämäläinen, offering counternarratives to the traditional stories of the colonial conquest of North America, illuminating the sophistication of Native American technologies and their flexible social organizations.

The authors of these books found an abundance of evidence from North America and around the world that our late-Paleolithic and Neolithic ancestors had sophisticated political imaginations. They were intentionally experimenting and developing new concepts for organizing communities and defining leadership with, it seems, a determination to keep dominant power from accumulating.

Some of the examples that intrigue me the most, that feed my optimism, are the people whose lives depended on the successful seasonal harvest and the preservation of their primary protein source—the maturing of a tree nut crop or a fish's migratory river run, for instance.

With a "life is on the line" goal of executing the most effective and efficient collecting and processing of the protein they depended on till the next season, they selected what I'll call a "big boss." And the big boss had a police force. They had the authority to make sure everyone had a role in the harvest or in the drying, mashing, smoking, curing, and preserving of the protein, and that they were delivering the needed performances consistently.

Then, when harvest time was over, the big boss and the police force lost their authority, returning to "civilian" status. That limitation on their authority—it's only temporarily theirs—shows how wise our ancestors were at building appropriately humane governing structures; knowing your power has a time limit and you'll return to live with those you policed, doesn't that make it much more likely you won't abuse your authority?

Around the world, there appear to have been a number of towns that grew so large that a permanent police force was put in place to maintain civil order. And the same beautiful wisdoms are shown; the police force was permanent, but a calendar rotation was set so the police force members would leave and a new group would take their place, often every six months.

The second guide prompt I offer is much shorter. This phrase hit me so hard as a complete idea that I figured I had read it somewhere. No search engine has found it for me, and I'm still not sure where it came from.

"Times of fierce cynicism demand a radical naivete."

My determination to maintain an optimistic approach to this work is fueled by this thought. Try it on as you read what comes next.

HOW COMMON GROUND FOR US SERVES ALL OF US

For decades before I suspected it might be Common Ground for US, I was actively exploring this creative common ground's energies and practices; its entrepreneurial behaviors and concepts; its generative ideas and processes; its fresh perspectives; and on and on, and all growing there in sustainable abundance. I've nurtured it and harvest regularly for workshops and classes and a weekly radio show, hoping to nourish each of us as we grow and act as our most creatively entrepreneurial selves.

Then one day, I shifted my perspectives just enough to see the outlines of something else, maybe something more. Each time I looked at it from a new angle, my interest grew, and I wondered if it was something that just might be what the nation needs, with our fierce divide and political language so weaponized as to be useless.

I took my radical naivete for a walk and found a bunch of strategies and stories that serve our country fully. They are listed here, then discussed one at a time:

1. Stories of the most rational and the most optimistic preparation for our future of unknowable unknowns
2. Common Wealth, a high-return strategy to leverage resources to benefit each and all of us
3. Numerous strategies supporting small businesses and entrepreneurs, the drivers of job growth and innovation
4. The promise of a grassroots renaissance when universal basic income arrives
5. New language for governance and fresh perspectives on systemic policy challenges
6. Stories becoming national narratives that unite us as natural-born creative geniuses growing into the most creative and entrepreneurial people, each capable of successfully making our way in this unknowable world, together achieving a sustainable abundance

1. Stories of the most rational and the most optimistic preparation for our future of unknowable unknowns

It's an act of leadership, telling these stories. They don't declare we should be united and then hope for it. They celebrate our natural unity, dramatizing how and demonstrating why it's vital.

In addition, these stories provide that powerful, productive energy, energy needed just as badly as national unity, and that's optimism.

Leaders know that telling a story once doesn't convey its significance. So they keep telling it, refreshing and extending it, continually developing spin-offs.

All of us living in the future that is present are trying to find a positive and productive vantage point for the future that is unknowable. What makes the future unknowable?

When I was teaching at Duke, I challenged students to imagine life just twenty years into the future; in 2005, they were imagining what life would be like in 2025. We discussed their ruminations and predictions two or three times over the course of the semester.

No one imagined two large and fiercely destructive changes to our culture, to our way of simply living a day.

No one predicted that playful childhood would be a tragic victim of the handheld computers Apple and others introduced just a couple of years later. No one imagined that, together with emerging online social platforms, these technologies would cause a dramatic decline in open-ended outdoor child's play and face-to-face socializing. Nor that these technologies would cause anxieties to spike, bullying too, and that empathy would shrivel. None of my students saw this coming.

And none of the students shared anything about our nation's democratic traditions and institutions being challenged at their foundations by a determined, focused, and purposely mean-spirited fight for power.

Today, this future that is present provides perspectives that help us understand the unknowable future's underlying dynamics.

- There will be constant unforeseen changes. This is true in the future that is present, and the unpredictable and complex nature of the changes will increase over the decades.
- There will be more fierce disruptions like the one we went through with COVID, except the next

disruption won't be anything like its predecessor; what we learned from our mistakes and successes last time may not be useful next time.

- And there will be incredible, unimaginable technology breakthroughs that will lead to waves and waves of unforeseeable opportunities, inviting new innovative ventures and supporting new ways to live sustainable lives abundantly.

Seeing within my calling a duty to help folks prepare for the unknowable future, I began to network with some futurists to listen to their professional consideration of the topic. Early on, one of them said that as they submit their ten-year forecast for a client—usually a municipality or large corporation—they make sure the client knows that "Our most likely scenario isn't very likely."

As you make your way in the face of the extraordinary challenges and unimaginable opportunities of the unknowable future, doesn't it seem the most rational preparation is developing your creatively entrepreneurial qualities, like those found rooted throughout Common Ground for US?

It's rational for you to become more adaptive, isn't it, to be more resilient, ingenious, inventive, collaborative, and curious; more adept at exploring and recognizing patterns and creating advantages for your families and communities and organizations.

And it's most optimistic because this most rational preparation plays to our strengths; we are all born with deep and broad creative abilities that grow with intention and application. You might even say we're all creative geniuses.

The majority of adults show high levels of anxiety when considering what comes next. A number of recent research projects show 75 percent of high school students express fear about the future, citing concerns about their career path, personal stability, climate change and the overall state of the world as contributing factors to their anxiety—isn't it likely the anxiety of their parents feeds theirs as well?

Sharing optimistic messages is a leader's opportunity to serve.

Political and community leaders' opportunities

When leaders tell their versions of a rationally optimistic story about preparing for the unknowable future, they do us a great service; they show genuine care and appreciation for what's to come. They assuage anxieties and fears. That's successful leadership—and they don't even have to be elected to serve us as storytellers.

Conservatives will be attracted to the self-reliance themes in these creative and entrepreneurial messages.

Progressives will appreciate the equity, the universal nature of this, and that creativity is a resource that grows when it is shared.

In the next section, you'll find short lessons on the creatively entrepreneurial concepts that are particularly important as we make our way in the unknowable future.

2. Common Wealth, a high-return strategy to leverage resources to benefit each and all of us

A common wealth's leverage of resources—we each benefit, we all benefit—is crucial for future flourishing, accomplishing sustainable abundance for all.

It's not a stealth introduction of socialism. It's this:

Ask ten first-time entrepreneurs if they want to launch

and build their businesses all by themselves or join a new-venture incubator where each of the founders brings their contacts, resources, and knowledge to share with the others, creating common wealth. My experience tells me you'd get nine out of ten, maybe even ten out of ten, choosing the common wealth of the incubator. They've either been told or know instinctively that their giving will be multiplied.

There's the Illinois farmer who won the blue ribbon at his county fair for the best sweet corn five years running; his success was noticed by a journalist, who arranged an interview. When asked about his secret for growing such a high-quality corn crop the farmer explained that when he harvests each year's crop, he collects the best of it for seed corn for next year and gives half of that prime seed corn to the farmers whose fields touch his. The journalist was confused and wondered why he was helping his potential competition. The farmer explained that when the breezes blow and the wind stirs, the pollen from neighboring fields floats on the currents of air to his fields and pollinates his crop.

So the best way to make sure his corn keeps improving was to help others improve theirs.

This historical example was labeled as socialism back when FDR set out to create jobs with large construction projects during the Great Depression. Let's look at just one of them, the Lincoln Tunnel, connecting New Jersey and Manhattan. This common wealth asset is owned by the people of New Jersey and New York. Is it possible to calculate the individual wealth, the private wealth, that has been facilitated by this shared public common wealth resource? How many small business owners have had more access to customers and vendors? How many friendships and cultural exchanges have been facilitated and nurtured? How many folks building their careers have benefited from more access to more opportunity? Measured on all scales of value creation and human benefits, is this common wealth's contribution incalculable?

Political and community leaders' opportunities

With a shared understanding of the generative nature and societal impact of common wealth, let's bring that understanding to discussing the importance of not just budgeting for public schools and libraries but investing in them as a community or neighborhood's common wealth.

A number of research projects—from the RAND Corporation to the National Bureau of Economic Research to the Annenberg Institute for School Reform—show conclusively that quality public schools contribute significantly to economic growth and community development. Improving educational outcomes leads to increasing property values, reduced crime, and fostering a skilled workforce. The studies show public schools play a key role in enhancing the economic vitality of their neighborhoods and communities.

Investing in makerspaces is a tremendous example of building common wealth. Adapted to local interests and budgets, makerspaces are work areas where creative folks—you and everyone else—have access to some combination of hand tools, materials, electronic components, sewing machines, laser cutters, power tools, looms, computers and design software, screen printing, and work benches.

And peer-to-peer learning and coaching.

Already, makerspaces are showing up in public schools—a presence making a positive impact for schoolchildren in their traditional studies—and in public libraries, where intergenerational learning is growing.

Their success collectively is quite impressive, considering many are poorly funded.

When makerspaces are added to schools, along with apprenticeships and other hands-on programs, students' performance in traditional subject areas improves, attendance improves, and disciplinary problems decrease.

We too often make the mistake of presuming that an education is consumed by students. Experienced educators know that students produce their education. These hands-on programs help students see themselves as producers, and they bring their new sense of self to all their work.

While makerspaces receive the focus in this book, there are other very important common wealth "innovation utilities" fostering collaborative creativity and entrepreneurship, individual advantage, and broad community benefits.

There are new-venture incubators, supporting entrepreneurs as they grow and launch new enterprises, creating jobs and delivering important new services and products to the public.

Public innovation centers are physical spaces usually affiliated with government agencies, universities, or corporations. They bring together citizens, entrepreneurs, and policymakers working collaboratively on solutions to civic challenges using technology, design thinking, and open data.

Community bio labs offer shared wet labs for citizen scientists and start-ups, providing access to equipment for synthetic biology, biohacking, or environmental testing.

Makerspaces will show up a couple more times later on. They are sweet-spot examples of how little it takes to nurture and enable the creative and entrepreneurial talents of the people, for the people, by giving the people access to resources and opportunities.

And the teacher in me wants to take a moment and

remind us that we are much more creative when we are working with our hands.

Conservatives will find very strong returns on investments growing common wealth programs in schools; truancy declines, student unemployment declines, and graduation rates rise, all signs of social health and well-being. One GOP-led apprenticeship program in Tennessee reduced teenage unemployment by 47 percent.

Progressives will appreciate the improvement in traditional academics that disadvantaged children show when involved in these sorts of programs. A makerspace program in California resulted in a 22 percent increase in female enrollment in physics classes.

3. Numerous strategies supporting small businesses and entrepreneurs, the major drivers of job growth and innovation.

This is a great example of how Common Ground for US leverages itself. All the creative and entrepreneurial strategies and behaviors that are found there are as vital to accomplishing healthy organizational growth as they are for our important personal growth. Entrepreneurs and business owners benefit when building their businesses in a region where folks are developing, expressing, and enjoying their own creative lives. A robust, creatively entrepreneurial ecosystem serves everyone, in every way.

The creative strategies and behaviors found in the next section are important for all of us and also serve leaders and builders of organizations. Highlighted here are a few concepts particularly important for business builders.

Ready Fire Aim (RFA) is a set of action strategies that has usefulness to all of us in limited situations, but are central to how entrepreneurs and business leaders approach new opportunities.

Successful experienced entrepreneurs don't start with a plan. They start by getting started.

They've learned that at the beginning, they don't know what will be most important to know for successful completion of the project, challenge, or opportunity. Rather than predict what the important thing will be, they discover it.

They, we, get smarter when we move, because now we're engaging all of our body's intelligences.

And we get smarter because we're moving into the problem and with it, taste testing the opportunity, getting smarter with each experience, with each step, even when it's a misstep.

Did you note the reordering of the common Ready Aim Fire? In the original, we've taken two steps and so far learned nothing. Ready Fire Aim means we take action sooner, to learn quickly; knowing more, our aim is much more effective the next time.

These RFA action steps help you think strategically to get the most out of your bias for action.

Fail fast, fail often, fail cheap

One more time, it's important: When we launch a venture or begin developing a new opportunity, let's keep in mind that we don't know the most important things we need to know about what we need to do to accomplish our goals or, in some instances, what those goals should be. That means we want to get smarter fast, and we especially want to build our own proprietary knowledge.

So we design informal, ad hoc experiments or trials or

tests that we can start quickly and complete quickly, to learn quickly.

Then we want another trial, another foray, refining each one with what we just learned, getting smarter at knowing what we are looking for.

And if we are going to fail often, we sure better fail cheap.

Do what you can with what you have where you are

What can be a cheaper, quicker, and lower-risk first step than seeing what you can do with what you already have, rather than delaying because you don't have all the resources you wanted?

Rosabeth Moss Kanter, a Harvard professor, has great ideas about leadership, including her insight that creative leaders engage in "kaleidoscopic thinking."

Her notion, right on point for us here, is that, just as a kaleidoscope creates a great variety of brand-new images without adding to the glass bits used, but by changing the relationships between the bits, we can rearrange the relationships between the resources we have on hand and often discover something new.

We need to intentionally overcome the trap of functional fixedness, a slice of status quo thinking, where we can only consider an object or situation in the way we've always considered it. Kaleidoscopic thinking is a great process for overcoming that trap.

Find friends fast

With a practice of being generous with your friends, you'll find they are ready to be generous in return. They will provide you with new perspectives on the challenge or opportunity—additional perspectives on this thing you are trying to figure out are particularly valuable in the early days of your venture.

And frequently, they will have access to resources they will share, including contacts with folks you'd like to meet, perhaps serving as or facilitating mini-tests of the idea.

Here's something you know, I'm just reminding you it's particularly useful in early stages: When you have to shape your thinking to share it with another, you will learn things about the idea you didn't know. Their reactions and then their questions tell you more.

Fish the confluences

In 1951, the construction of the Bull Shoals Dam on the White River in the Arkansas Ozarks was completed. It's the waters from the depths of Bull Shoals Lake, 58 degrees, often cooler, that feed the White River and transformed it from a southern warm-water river to a cold coolness just right, it was soon discovered, for rainbow and brown trout to thrive.

When I guided on the White in 1969 and 1970, soon after we were back on the river following a stony shoal shore lunch, we'd come to the wide expanse of the Buffalo River flowing into the White. The Buffalo River was the first river to be designated a National Wild River, and its warmer oxygen-rich waters offer great smallmouth bass fishing.

There in the confluences, where the Buffalo's warm thermal layers with the White's cold, the fish that are only found in one river—no trout in the Buffalo, no bass in the White—were together there in abundance, the waters teeming with the life that fuels theirs, great varieties of minnows and crustaceans and other water critters drawn to this place.

Where ecosystems overlap, life flourishes. Where demographic groups interact, innovation flourishes. Where disciplines merge, genius flourishes. Where ideas converge, opportunity flourishes. Find those places and hang out. Before you study those places, get a feel for them, get used to them, wander and wonder.

Political and community leaders' opportunities

Invest in the high-leverage common wealth of business incubators, makerspaces, wet labs, and innovation centers that provide vital tools for ingenious and imaginative individuals to develop new skills and collaborate with others to launch new ventures. These facilities also attract diverse communities and set the stage for intergenerational learning,

Mitch Kapor, a pioneer in the tech world, shared an insight that should fuel all that we do here: "Talent is equally distributed across all zip codes, opportunity is not." The same is true for resources.

Common Ground for US brings new creative language and entrepreneurial justifications to support the moral argument that this gap must not stand.

Experienced entrepreneurs know there's opportunity, investing in and cultivating undervalued assets—an investment approach brings with it a commitment to, and much smarter thinking about, developing talent—so a leadership strategy that puts a high priority on starting common wealth facilities in underserved communities will pay off as common wealth will, serving individuals and communities.

Conservatives and progressives appreciate the messages of self-reliance and the celebration of, and support for, programs that offer opportunities for sustained entrepreneurial growth.

4. The promise of a grassroots renaissance when universal basic income arrives

Is it inevitable that there will be a national universal basic income (UBI)? If there is, it will further leverage the radical nature of the changes in the economy that called for it. And since so many of us build activities and habits, including decisions about where we live, around the schedule and demands of our work, isn't it likely that there can be radical changes in how we get to organize a day and invest our time as we drive this grassroots renaissance?

I can't predict when UBI arrives, but there is good reason to anticipate it will. Here in our future that is present, the changes that will drive a UBI are happening fast, and all signs indicate they won't be slowing down.

1. When businesses replace jobs with AI and other technologies, they are reducing their largest operating expense: personnel costs, including salaries, wages, and benefits. This can be as much as 70 percent of a business's expenses, so profits grow significantly when jobs are eliminated.
2. A time will arrive when such a large number of folks will be unemployed that the market's purchasing power will be seriously eroded.
3. Businesses need a market to sell their goods and services so they can continue to generate their high profits.
4. Businesses' support for a tax to fund a UBI that puts money in folks' pockets will not just be good

> business; it will become necessary to do business.
> Can you imagine seeing the Chamber of Commerce lobbying for this on behalf of their members?
> Won't surprise me.

A creative leader can radically change the conversation about what happens when UBI is instituted. Standing alone, this stipend is vulnerable to claims that, no matter how necessary, it's just a welfare program or government overreach. It is often called that now in political discussions.

When UBI is preceded by leaders' commitment to helping us all grow our natural creative and entrepreneurial qualities, the stipend can be positioned authentically as an investment helping makers make, creators create, builders build, and growers grow.

So here I am, please note the frequency, again advocating investment in common wealth facilities like incubators and makerspaces. Because . . .

"If you want to teach people a new way of thinking, don't bother trying to teach them. Instead, give them a tool, the use of which will lead to new ways of thinking."

That's from Buckminster Fuller (1895-1983), the architect and engineer, designer and inventor, and futurist. You'll find my thoughts on the controversy that has arisen recently about Fuller-the-man in the section titled A Bit About My Politics.

A while back, a makerspace fair was taking place down the road, so I attended. The booths were buzzing, and new connections were happening. I followed a crowd to listen to a panel of advocates for the growing movement, and they provided a bunch of numbers establishing clearly that these innovation utilities are proving to have a positive impact on local and regional economies.

The numbers were impressive, but what stuck with me were the stories they all told about walking the floors at other makerspace conventions and fairs and hearing time and time again some version of "I mean, that part kept wearing out so fast I figured I'd make my own. Then I discovered others need that part, and before I knew it, I was in business for myself."

I go to bed imagining what will happen when we've been investing in our creative capital, we've been investing in common wealth facilities like makerspaces, and then along comes UBI. What can you imagine would happen?

Political and community leaders' opportunities

Conservatives understand this approach to UBI sustains markets and reduces welfare bureaucracy, letting free enterprise build.

Progressives appreciate this approach to UBI, ensuring AI's profits are invested in grassroots innovations, small business development, community building, and, therefore, human dignity, not just billionaire wealth.

5. New language for governance and fresh perspectives on systemic policy challenges.

Rooted in Common Ground for US we find language and behaviors for a productive renewal of governance. When we are honest about the damage that has been done to current political language, so weaponized that it's of no productive value, we realize we must find new language and behaviors so we can build paths to more promising, productive places, paths that make the walls separating us irrelevant and eventually historical ruins.

A personal admission: This particular idea, that creativity can infuse our political language and behaviors, is where my naivete is most radical. I hope we'll aspire to reclaim the political imaginations our ancestors showed, for tens of thousands of years, all around our planet.

Political and community leaders' opportunities

When policy debate turns to public schools and libraries, leaders who create advantage will shift the nature of the debate to include the reports of the extraordinary individual and community benefits that occur when these places are treated as opportunities to invest.

As opportunities to invest in growing high-leverage community-centered common wealth.

Leaders should bring an investment mindset to growing and improving our common wealth. We care about what we invest in, we nurture our assets, and we measure the returns of our investments. A clear-eyed approach to the financial returns from investing in students' educations, along with attempts to quantify other individual and community benefits, makes a conclusive case for continued investments in public schools and libraries.

It's a smart strategy to keep investing where you enjoy a great rate of return. A 2023 study determined that every $1 invested in a public-school makerspace yielded $12 in growth for the local economy.

A very important opportunity to shift political debate and policy making is to be clear about the difference between "taking advantage" of an opportunity and "creating advantage" from an opportunity.

Do we harvest what's there or grow more? Do we take the best and leave the rest, or do we nourish and nurture?

This shift in perspectives would have a role in tax policy. It shows why investments in new ventures, in new innovative technologies, and in medical and green-tech R&D will be taxed very favorably; these investments create advantages through cascading benefits for many while potentially improving the quality of life for all. Speculative investments that only profit the individual investor will receive less-favorable tax treatment; the longer an investment is held, the more favorable the tax treatment, generally.

Affordable housing and the unhoused are related policy areas that benefit from Common Ground for US perspectives on governance.

For instance, when we bring a create advantage approach to policy making in this area, we design and test programs of subsidies and tax advantages to support and reward developers and home builders for building low-income and climate-smart houses. It's another place where astute investment not only helps a few directly but the whole community, and in important ways.

When real estate investors acquire enough of an area's housing stock to raise rents or run them as Airbnb-type short-term rentals (STRs), housing options for families diminish and become more expensive, hurting the larger community as well.

There are a number of different approaches to keep residential housing speculation of the sort that hurts communities at bay.

There could be tax breaks for landlords who convert their STRs to workforce housing; too often, public employees can't afford to live in the areas they serve.

Some municipalities have been trying ideas like higher taxes on STRs when they exceed a certain percentage of the total housing stock. New Orleans taxes profits from STRs at a higher rate than long-term leases and uses that tax revenue to fund affordable housing.

Conservatives appreciate the self-reliance and producer spirit of makerspaces and the community benefits of quality public schools. They will see how local communities care for themselves best when affordable housing is sufficient.

Progressives appreciate providing tools and resources to those who couldn't otherwise afford them. They will rise to help communities protect themselves from rampant speculation.

6. Stories becoming national narratives that unite us as natural-born creative geniuses, growing into the most creative and entrepreneurial people, each of us capable of successfully making our way in this unknowable world, all of us achieving a sustainable abundance together

The political leadership power of stories is undeniable. In 1704, Andrew Fletcher, the Scottish writer, politician, and patriot, wrote, "If a man were permitted to write all the ballads, he need not care who should make the laws of a nation."

The power Fletcher ascribes to ballads—narratives with music—holds true for stories. We need to, we love to, understand the world through stories we tell and are told, sung and spoken. We understand ourselves through the stories we tell to ourselves and to those who listen.

If you were given the chance to develop the narrative shaping the way a community thinks about itself, the way they choose to govern themselves will be true to that narrative.

Common Ground for US supports a national aspirational story that calls on each of us to participate in creating a sustainable abundance for all of us.

An aspirational story has three parts:

1. It identifies challenges to overcome to build a better-than-before future.
2. It dramatizes, rationalizes, and even lionizes a boldly better-than-before future.
3. It narrates and illustrates the behaviors that help us create and discover that better-than-before future.

The national unity and the creative and entrepreneurial qualities that Common Ground for US offers—the best of our creative and entrepreneurial behaviors, skills, and energies—are ready now. Ready for leaders to shape the aspirational narrative that is true to the future that is present, that offers a flourishing and fulfilling future, and illustrates ways to get us there.

Earlier in the book, I called upon Charles Mingus to illustrate the point that it's helpful—or was he saying it was necessary?—to share a suggestion, some direction, some sort of first offer that helps us start thinking about the topic at hand.

As a new-venture builder my usual was to bring to the table a very early draft of a strategy for a new initiative or a rough tactical plan for an opportunity, inviting the team to make my offering theirs, because once it's theirs they do what they will with it—improve it, learn what they can then toss it aside, integrate it, and, I discovered, often making it better in ways I hadn't imagined.

I am not developing an aspirational story here; stories

must be alive with the details relevant to the time, the place, and people, calling for specific actions needed for then and there. Instead, I am sharing some tools, maybe something of a template, for leaders to design their own aspirational stories that call for an all-hands-on-deck national mission to achieve a sustainable abundance for everyone.

1. An aspirational story is rooted in a shared understanding of the future that is present, in a form others recognize as true.

That's vital. The story's journey requires a generally accepted understanding at the start of it. Certainly, leaders will select those examples of the future that is present that best sets the stage for the story they are planning to tell, but the examples must be presented honestly and accurately.

In the future that is present, well, there's no other way to put it: We hate each other. Once upon a time, the two major parties viewed the other as the loyal opposition and worked together. Now each thinks the other side is immoral. Political leadership, at best, accepts this and too often feeds fearful hate. I'm an optimist, and the data measuring our hate is frightening.

Current political language has been so weaponized as to be useless in helping useful political conversation progress.

Politicians show very little to suggest they are being thoughtful on our behalf about how the country should be preparing, right now and from now on, for an unknowable future.

The economy is fragile. A system that primarily benefits the already successful isn't thriving; it's closer to plundering, resulting in an economy where 60 percent of us live paycheck to paycheck.

Our planet is burning. Politicians seem incapable of understanding the magnitude of the challenge and maintaining any urgency to act.

And foundational to any aspirational story's beginning—the journey's origin story—is the celebration of the underlying common ground truth that we have always been, and continue to be, extraordinarily creative and entrepreneurial people, capable of accomplishing any challenge, ready to lead a grassroots revival and renew existing organizations. This optimistic truth becomes a character in the story and the tenor of the journey.

2. An aspirational story dramatizes a future better than before, of sustainable abundance, and calls on us to achieve it.

The aspirational story must excite us. It must be demanding the best of each of us, promising a life that is boldly better than anything we've experienced, like a sustainable abundance for all.

Using simple logic with emotional engagement will help folks hold the story easily in their minds and their hearts and souls.

JFK's aspirational challenge to travel to the moon is often captured in these words from his speech at Rice University: "We choose to go to the moon. We choose to go to the moon in this decade and do the other things, not because they are easy, but because they are hard . . ."

The words that immediately follow are spot on.

". . . because that goal will serve to organize and measure the best of our energies and skills, because that challenge is one that we are willing to accept, one we are unwilling to postpone, and one which we intend to win . . ." Do you love it? That this test, this challenge, calls us to be better than before?

An aspirational story's better-than-before future balances individual accomplishment and national success; we each have an important role and contribution to make the bold promise of sustainable abundance real, and we all benefit when we do. The story will illustrate each of us flourishing as we capably make our way regardless of what comes our way.

And the story celebrates our unity, showing us working together, applying our creative and entrepreneurial abilities, as we make our way in the future of unknowns, each day getting closer to the big, bold goal of achieving a sustainable abundance for all.

3. It narrates and illustrates the journey from now to then, highlighting behaviors that help us discover and create the best versions of our bold goal.

There are two sources of creative energy and entrepreneurial behaviors needed for this journey. There's bottom-up self-organization—the healthiest, most sustainable growth—and there's top-down sources of needed resources.

Bottom-up self-organization

The foundation for all the stories portraying us preparing for the unknowable future and achieving our sustainable abundance aspirations is the Common Ground for US stories of creative genius 98 percent of us share. Remember: this common ground is attractive to the cultural and political left and right; it's useful for rural and small town folks, for suburban and urban residents; it serves those who already have and those who don't have yet; it's important to old folks and, it's pretty clear, it's even more important for those living deep into this century.

A leader's "how we get there" stories are rooted in and nurtured by this creative common ground. The stories will be ripe with vignettes and through lines of our common ground's importance to our flourishing fulfillment as we make our way toward achieving a sustainable abundance in the unknowable future.

Perhaps leaders will find offering this journey as patriotic is an appealing message—that a commitment to personal creative growth, and to helping others grow as well, is fundamental to our nation's future vitality. The messages will share reminders that there is no future for any of us unless there is a future for all of us.

The stories will call for and celebrate local investment in common wealth resources and facilities, reminding us how the concept of common wealth serves individuals and communities, and that common wealth delivers the greatest returns from resources, crucial to attaining a sustainable abundance.

Stories of the benefits of investing in common wealth makerspaces, new-venture incubators, wet labs, and innovation centers, the development of co-ops and employee-owned businesses, portray individual and community benefits. Effective stories reiterate the key role that investing in public schools and libraries plays.

Stories will share case studies of common wealth delivering the greatest returns from resources, crucial to attaining a sustainable abundance. Others will illustrate early successes where "create advantage" tax policy is working: the development of promising new technologies like carbon extraction; communities where home builders have long wait-lists of buyers for their green homes; teenagers growing community gardens to feed the elderly; mentoring and tutoring and apprenticeship programs.

The UBI stories of this journey will position the stipend as an investment in the productive abilities of a creative and entrepreneurial people, calling for and celebrating the grassroots renaissance.

And the stories of our journey will examine and highlight the many innovative pedagogies proven to help students become producers of their education, developing creative skills as they learn, acquiring new understandings and knowledge of traditional subject matter most effectively.

The creativity that public school teachers have long displayed as they've done what they can with what little they have is another important storyline. Teachers will be continually recruited and celebrated as important servant leaders in these stories.

It's interesting physics, eh, that when the first political leaders begin telling their versions of these stories, it distinguishes them and unites us.

Top-down sources of needed resources

In 2024, the RAND Corporation study *The Fates of Nations* identified the factors that, historically, have caused great nations to decline. Many of those factors are associated with "elites" separating themselves from the greater community and dismissing any sense of responsibility to help others prosper.

The RAND study examines the erosion of trust in institutions—"truth decay," they call it—and proposes a framework for Anticipatory National Renewal (ANR), urging elite-driven reforms in governance, media, and education to prevent societal collapse. Why elite-driven? The study warns that if elites aren't successfully recruited to ANR being in their self-interest, it is likely they will oppose the reforms needed.

The study addresses the role of corporations in our renewal, finding it both critical and problematic. They praise the private sector's efficiency and scaling capacity while noting the problems inherent in their short-term fixation, and call for innovative "public-private partnerships."

The study concludes that our country is still in the "recoverable zone," but edging closer to the cliff.

While the study doesn't explicitly call out the successes of the 1950s through the 1980s, when the federal government invested aggressively in core R&D like DARPA and NASA and the Interstate Highway System, it promotes the model; Common Ground for US calls for it specifically and enthusiastically.

The stories would tell of the tremendous returns we all enjoyed from those investments, as 50 percent of the growth in our economy from 1945 to 2000 was driven by federal R&D investment. DARPA had a foundational role in the development of the internet, GPS, mRNA vaccine technologies, and lots more.

In the face of recent years of reduced investment—federal investment in core R&D has been cut by more than half—the Common Ground for US stories call for an increase in federal R&D investment, pointing out that the investments will be even more effective with our country's grassroots creative renewal.

A nation of creatively entrepreneurial people would be more agile in adopting the sorts of systemic changes the RAND Study calls for, more capable of spotting flaws and adapting in real time, more likely to view "anticipatory national renewal" not as a bureaucratic challenge, but as a mission.

The stories advocate for favorable tax rates for investments in technologies key to us achieving a sustainable abundance. So investments in green tech—with a priority focus on carbon removal—will be supported with the lowest tax rates.

Allow a musical paraphrase of Bob Dylan:

"A nation not busy being born is busy dying."

HARMONIZING SUSTAINABILITY WITH ABUNDANCE

OUR COUNTRY HAS THE KNOWLEDGE, TECHNOLOGY, and financial and human creative capital to achieve a sustainable abundance for each of us, for all of us, even as we face the challenges of an unknowable future. It should be, it must be our generation's all hands-on-deck moon shot, and that means we won't accomplish it, we can't even start it, unless we root the discussions, the planning, the investment, in Common Ground for US.

This might be the most important example of Common Ground for US uniting by inviting new ways to talk about, to think about, traditional political divides. One political view is all in on abundance, on unleashing our innovative energies to build and create, often dismissing sustainability advocacy as anti-growth. The view committed to sustainability demands that attention be paid to what we have done and are doing to the natural world, offering strategies for restoring health, too often minimizing the importance of growth and making it more difficult.

Here, with the application of the power of both, they no

longer defend against each other; they lock arms with each other.

Since the founding of our nation, creativity and entrepreneurship have replaced scarcity with abundance, transforming the lives of many millions for the better. And that extraordinary transformation has resulted in serious damage to our home.

Creating a sustainable abundance will require committed and collective innovation. We need new inventions, we need new approaches for living together.

And let's reclaim old approaches for business, government, and unions to work together like they did so effectively during most of the second half of the 1900s, creating an economy that innovated and lifted, not one that harvested with little returned.

NASA had no idea how they were going to meet JFK's challenge—they lacked the technical knowledge, they had no experienced strategic insight, so they got started learning and discovering and learning some more.

We will learn a lot from NASA's approach, knowing the solutions are there; all it takes is a unified, creatively entrepreneurial, full-on commitment to discover them.

COMMUNITY SERVICE CLUBS: POWERFUL CREATIVE COMMON WEALTH

WITH THE HIGHEST REGARD FOR THE ROLE community service clubs have played for many decades, and with optimism they'll find the best leadership role for them to take on here, I wanted to place this section as close to the middle of the book as I could, seeing this as kinda sorta maybe its beating heart; it's pretty close, eh?

Rotary, Lions, Kiwanis, Optimist, and other clubs are extraordinary hubs of creative common wealth. Their networks—rooted in well-earned trust and hands-on problem-solving—could help seed a grassroots national renaissance by:

1. Building intergenerational creativity: Pairing retired experts with young entrepreneurs in makerspaces or civic labs, turning wisdom into generative fuel. And what a great community service project it would be to start new innovation utilities.
2. Adopting public schools as creativity incubators: Sponsoring creativity workshops where students tackle real town challenges (empty storefronts?

aging infrastructure?), blending service with skill building.

3. Scaling their community service spirit to host local "Common Ground Festivals," where left and right unite around fun and productive activities—creativity workshops and labs, with storytelling, music, and the arts. Recruiting Braver Angels —the national organization committed to improving communications and understanding between the politically divided—to join the festivals could lead to more robust relationships between a club and this organization, serving both as they serve us.

As Common Ground for US illustrates, creativity thrives in connection. These clubs are woven with rich, diverse, and creative connective tissue. Recruiting one or more would be a powerful momentum builder for these ideas.

In the early days of writing this book, I had the opportunity to share early versions of some of these ideas at lunchtime talks to four service clubs. First, I got to listen in on the club's business meeting with updates on their work, and wow, it is inspiring to see the enthusiasm members have to serve their local communities in dozens of important ways. I met members who'd actively participated in service programs for thirty years.

HELPING ALL OF US PREPARE

I AM CAPTURED BY MY CALLING, A DELIGHTED prisoner. Since 2002, I have been studying the what and practicing the how of helping folks develop their creative and entrepreneurial qualities. And tracking the why it's so important finds that importance growing steadily.

From the vantage point that the future that is present provides, selected here are the creative concepts, entrepreneurial behaviors, and strategies that will be particularly effective in helping you prepare to make your way facing an unknowable future and helping us all achieve a sustainable abundance. At the start of the book, I stated I have reasons for repeating ideas and content, and you'll find that here; my expectation is you will think about the creative ideas differently the second or third time you read them.

THE THREE PRINCIPLES OF A CREATIVELY ENTREPRENEURIAL MINDSET

After a couple of semesters teaching, I began looking for some way to organize what I was doing—my experience as an entrepreneur taught me that a search for structures will often result in fresh insight into the relationships of pieces and parts.

From the beginning, the Three Principles of a Creatively Entrepreneurial Mindset have held true. They are part of each other and feed all the creative and entrepreneurial qualities we find on Common Ground for US.

1. Be intentionally creatively entrepreneurial

Since we are born creative geniuses, all you have to do is intentionally embrace the importance of being your most creatively entrepreneurial self—declare it to yourself, reveal your plans to develop your creativity to your family and friends—and you won't be disappointed.

In fact, a very important early success is promised. You see, the 4 P professions—poets and psychologists, physicists and philosophers—all agree from their radically different professional perspectives that we don't see the world the way it is, we see it the way we are.

So when you embrace that this is who you are, when you cultivate the most creative and entrepreneurial version of yourself, you begin to see the world the way a creative and entrepreneurial person sees the world.

It's most likely that your initial changes in perspectives will be incremental. Please note, I didn't write "just incremental," for often great creative usefulness is found in the increment. If you see a problem or an opportunity a little bit differently today than yesterday, it might offer the perspectives that provide insight for progress.

2. Bias for action

We are smarter when we move. In fact, we're smarter times two.

There are a number of theories, including somatic intelligence and embodied cognition, that help us understand the nature of the intelligences distributed throughout our body. They all agree our intelligences are only fully engaged when we move, resulting in better creative idea generation and better problem solving.

And since we're moving, why not head to the neighborhood where the problem hangs out or the opportunities reside? Let's interact with their space, getting used to it and them.

You want to understand something new? First get used to it, then study it.

2. Multiple creative perspectives

Yes, two number "2s"; their dance together is inevitable and just about continuous.

Throughout my entrepreneurial career, I thought the status quo I was fighting against was "out there," in tradition and hierarchy and bureaucracy. And it is.

But the most formidable status quo challenge is our brains. Offering up the status quo angle or view or thought is our brains' favorite shortcut; it works twenty-four seven, and sending us down the same neuro pathways it's been using in a particular circumstance is, well, the least it can do.

We need to intentionally bust the bonds of the familiar so we can look at what is happening, not what we expect will happen. We accomplish that by taking lots of perspectives on the challenge. Different times. Different approaches. Sometimes alone, sometimes with a friend. When you're happy. When you're sad.

And since it is a numbers game, exercise your "bias for action" and get started now. The best way to acquire useful insights into the future of unknowns is to actively explore.

FIFTEEN CREATIVE CONCEPTS

Be generous

You read about the creative power of generosity earlier and have no doubt experienced it yourself many times. When you are generous to someone, they are highly likely to be generous in return. Perhaps they reciprocate in the moment, perhaps days later, and maybe it's another benefiting from your generous act.

Be generous with all the new ideas and changes the unknowable future tosses at you. Make the best case you can for them; you'll learn so much more than if you reject them immediately. And your generous consideration means you're more confident in your acceptance or rejection of the change.

My recommendation is that you bring a generous approach to life daily, generally, intentionally; it builds creative energies and opportunities all around. Then, when you are focused on a project, make certain that focus includes your most generous perspectives and behaviors.

Be humble

This was an important creative behavior in the past. It's an important creative behavior in the future that is present. Does it quickly become clear that humility will be even more important in the unknowable future?

No doubt you can be humble in your person and still quite proud of your accomplishments. Don't you find genuinely humble people getting excited about the piece of work they just created very attractive?

We won't know the most important things we'll need to know when we start a new project or make our way in different times. So, embrace that there will be a whole lot of "I don't know," wisely followed by "What do you think?"

The beginning of wisdom is wonder, and the beginning of wonder is awe. If you are sure you know, will you be curious? Will you wonder? We'll need new wisdoms to replace the many that will be outmoded.

Again, Buckminster Fuller:

> I am enthusiastic over humanity's extraordinary and sometimes very timely ingenuity. If you are in a shipwreck and all the boats are gone, a piano top buoyant enough to keep you afloat that comes along makes a fortuitous life preserver. But this is not to say that the best way to design a life preserver is in the form of a piano top. I think that we are clinging to a great many piano tops in accepting yesterday's fortuitous contrivings as constituting the only means for solving a given problem.

Be playful

First of all, and I forget to stress this sometimes, being playful is fun. Let's always be on watch for fun, its own reward.

The practical creative benefits of being playful are where I usually start; they're good ones.

It's a great refresh. Open-ended play—starting a game with who and what is on hand where you find yourself making up rules and objectives as you go along, and often enough changing them—is a fun and effective creative work-out. You have to be adaptive. Resilient. Collaborative. Adept at pattern recognition. You develop those qualities by playing with them.

Children engaged in open-ended play discover and create imaginative narratives, engage in rapid prototyping as a stick is a sword until it's broken in half to be a telescope, and show strategic nimbleness as the game changes to include others. And children playing on the playground show more discipline than they do in the classroom.

Lots of research supports what you already know: We learn faster and retain more when there is a playful quality to the learning opportunities. A dopamine release is triggered by play, improving focus, memory consolidation, and retention.

Playing stimulates the brain's ability to reorganize itself—that wonderful quality of neuroplasticity, your brain becoming what you are asking it to be—essential for learning.

It's also a great way to get fresh perspectives on your challenge when, at some point in your exploration, you are intentionally playful. Plus, being playful means you are likely enjoying your exploration, so you aren't in a hurry and will take the time needed for new perspectives to emerge; you keep getting used to it.

Enthusiastically searching for beauty

Please, yes please, intentionally look for the beautiful. Look for it always. All ways. What do you think is beautiful? Where do you find it? What's the experience?

Does its beauty offer a sacred calm so you float along? Does it thunder a demand for response you're eager to give?

Regardless of your sense of beauty, it's a complex of patterns, shapes, harmonies, energies, textures, colors, and sounds, and when you experience the deep, rich, beautiful complexity, your subconscious mind is absorbing it all, cataloging, mashing, appending, and in various ways preparing it all for future creative needs.

We all know how important it is to refresh our digital devices. It's even more important to refresh your body, mind, and soul, and to simply behold what you consider beautiful, to just be present, is a great refresh.

As I mentioned with Being Generous, I try to intentionally act true to these four behaviors throughout my day, and then when I am working on a project, I bring these behaviors to that challenge.

A bonus: Research shows your peripheral vision widens when you are in a good mood, and it's always made sense to me that if I am some combo of being generous, humble, playful, and enthusiastic about beauty, that I am likely to be in the best mood the other circumstances of my life permit.

What a great asset in a constantly changing world, to see more of it, which leads to . . .

Pattern recognition

Our ability to locate the first incomplete outlines of emerging qualities of the future that is unknown; that will serve us well.

Pattern recognition can be an analytical practice. You study the data, the information, and you find a disconnect or an anomaly and start exploring what is causing it and what that teaches you.

And it can be intuitive. Again, my recommendation is that before you apply your analytical abilities, you first get used to it. Our brains work much better when we have a sense of the whole before we attend to the details. You want to spend time living in a forest, breathing its nature, before you study the trees.

Bring a friend into your pattern recognition activities—perhaps you could each focus on different domains. And since neuroscience finds that our brains' natural abilities to detect patterns—"fluid intelligence"—is at its best in our twenties through forties, if you are older than that, bring a young friend or family member.

Practice your pattern recognition skills. Look for patterns in license plates, phone numbers, addresses, or street names. Listen for trends in topics folks talk about. When you walk and wander in the woods, you live with the patterns of nature; your subconscious mind's constant alertness locates them.

Research found that simple Match 3 online video games have a positive impact on your pattern recognition abilities. I take fifteen minutes at some point in my day to play a couple of rounds.

In my teenage fishing guide days, working and living with Ojibway First Nations friends, I heard their appreciation for a special sort of wisdom: understanding the patterns of nature that promise abundance and learning to live in harmony with those patterns. Can you dig it?

Story

One of the most powerful qualities of story is that we all know how it works. If I led a two-hour workshop on story, I believe folks would be nodding their heads and saying to themselves, "Yeah, I guess I knew that" much of the time.

Does it help you to consider story as the one and only universal knowledge management technology?

We all are storytellers—so it is universal—and story brings context and emotion to information that invites a knowledgeable understanding and greater retention. Research reveals that first developing an emotional structure for a topic makes it much more likely that the facts will be retained.

It's simply one more technology to master—let's consider story's many forms to be mental software and its content data storage—and you've mastered many technologies, so be confident here too.

When you share information with someone, it is processed in a limited part of their brains, the language processing regions. When you wrap that same information in a narrative, the listener's brain is fully engaged, including the areas processing emotion. Plus, a little shot of dopamine occurs.

Earlier, you read the view of Andrew Fletcher, the Scottish patriot, about the power of the ballads a nation sings in shaping public life and opinion. It's a graceful transition to say the same about story controlling the narrative that influences what a community, small or large, expects of itself.

As you study patterns emerging and the creative energies driving them, if you discover a narrative that helps folks understand what's happening and you share it, you are serving. And the most useful way to serve keeps the narrative open-ended, ready and able to double back or take a new approach or add contributions from others.

One of the most effective ways to attract and maintain someone's attention is by telling them a story that is important to them, their story, one that shows an authentic understanding of their lives, their hopes. With their attention, your story tells how you will help make their story even better.

A story, both prepared and spontaneous, will include people, tension or conflict, surprises, timelines, successes, and a more-is-coming promise. Not every story needs all these story elements, especially when you are crafting one for the moment.

Liminal space and time

"Liminal" comes from the Latin *limen*, meaning "threshold." A threshold is where transitions begin—you step from outdoors to indoors. Sometimes the transition is that quick, and sometimes there's a foyer of sorts, a place that's in between, where you are no longer outside, where you have a moment to prepare for what's inside.

A monarch, in the chrysalis, is no longer what it was and not yet what it will be—it resides in liminal space. A graduation ceremony marks transition—let's celebrate your grade school accomplishments as we invite you to see yourself as something new, someone else.

Liminal space and time are filled with ambiguity. My wife's management of threshold transitions in the Waldorf preschool she started and ran for nearly twenty years served her students well by minimizing that ambiguity. She designed the physical environment so that the kids arrived in their family's cars with Mom and Dad as children of their family. They'd walk down a flagstone walk toward the brick wall and school gate, an archway covered with flowering vines. Marie, my wife, was waiting for the kids just outside the gate, where she greeted them, said goodbye to the parents, and walked them through the gate and down the river-stone gravel path that led them into the new place, the different place, the magic schoolyard, the children ready—usually eager—to be who they get to be while living in that world.

Try to be certain about this: are you running from or running toward? As you find yourself in between, are you there because you want to go to a new destination, or because you have to leave the old one? Or both?

Having friends' support and perspectives is valuable. When the liminal time is long or the space is wide, finding threads of an open-ended narrative to help you understand, and perhaps even guide you, is valuable.

Jazz musicians turn ambiguity into beauty by first being prepared, then staying open to something new, something else.

Social capital

Your social capital is your network of friends and family, associates and colleagues, with whom you have a relationship. It never hit me until I was working on this book that each social capital network is a dynamic common wealth association: You share your contacts and knowledge with others in your network, and members of your network share the same with you; your benefits are leveraged when you invest your social capital.

Research has shown that the person with the most robust social capital network—one that is large and diverse—is most likely to come up with the most creatively practical solution for the problem or strategy for the opportunity.

The most effective way to build your social capital network is by being generous with others. By sharing your contacts and introducing those who'll benefit from knowing each other. By alerting folks to new opportunities. By sharing a book, article, or website you know they would enjoy. And generosity's wonderfully reciprocal nature—generosity most often gets a generous response—results in your social capital network being filled with folks ready to be generous in return.

As important as your social capital network is in the future that is present, it will only grow in importance in the unknowable future. You benefit from more vantage points, more diverse sounding boards, more sources for needed resources, and perhaps earlier signals of significant changes. These serve you so well in liminal times.

Communications

One of the easiest places to practice your intentionality is giving the greatest gift we can give in the future that is present and in the unknowable future: your undivided attention. And it's a gift for both of you when you listen appreciatively—when you listen for the very best of what your friend or colleague is saying.

When someone knows they are being heard, they feel respected, perhaps even honored, and will be more inclined to share the best of what they have with you—you've begun recruiting them into your social capital network. Your close, appreciative listening to the ideas—the shapes and forms and patterns of them—results in them being integrated into your creative subconscious.

Your care-filled listening results in you collecting more of those dots Steve Jobs urged us to collect—you'll recall his understanding of creativity is simply connecting the dots, so make sure you have lots of dots. When your reputation spreads as an appreciative listener, you'll find yourself well-positioned to learn about the ideas percolating around you.

Since you have been listening appreciatively, doesn't it seem most likely that the first things you will say will come from that place of appreciation, that you will say appreciative things? Sometimes that results in the idea appreciating, which is pretty cool.

Now that you've shown genuine appreciation for the idea, now that the two of you are standing on a common ground of appreciation, now you can critique the idea, and now the speaker will hear it, knowing it's coming from someone who respects the idea. That's pretty cool too.

As the world becomes something else, we need to be thoughtful about the words we use to describe what's happening. We know our thoughts shape our words; let's be mindful that our words shape our subsequent thinking. What we call something has a huge impact on how we think about it.

We speak roughly sixteen thousand words a day. That's fertile ground for generating creative energy when, just two or three times a day, we intentionally select words that invite, that are open-ended. You invite a much more interesting energy into the room when, instead of asking a friend, "Did you enjoy your evening?" which can be answered yes or no, you ask, "What did you enjoy about your evening?"

A favorite example of being mindful in our use of language: Doesn't it seem that when we spot a new opportunity, we will almost automatically say, "Hmm, I wonder how I can take advantage of this opportunity?" Now, that doesn't necessarily mean you will take the best and leave the rest, but it points our thinking in that direction, if only incrementally.

What happens to your thinking if you were to say, "I wonder how I can create advantage from this opportunity." Once again, it doesn't necessarily mean you will nurture it, care for it, invite others to come and work on it together, but, at least incrementally, using that language directs your thinking that way.

In the unknowable future, there will be challenging situations where we have the opportunity to carefully select the best language for the new situation. When COVID arrived and we were told we'd be better off if we respected and maintained six feet of social distancing, did you quickly realize that was the wrong language creating the wrong story?

First, it wasn't accurate. They wanted six feet of physical distancing.

Second, it seems at times of physical distancing we need conversations about how to create more social engagement, more social coherence. But our leaders couldn't call for it because social was misapplied and not available for its best use.

The power of both

As you make your way in the unknowable future of unpredictable and sometimes radical changes, and you're looking for promising patterns and evidence of sustainable abundance, you'll likely bump into times when you find two contradictory directions, interpretations, or ideas.

Before you compromise or reject one, try out the power of both.

It was taught to me by two baby snapping turtles. One early Sunday morning, I found them crossing a country road, low swampy woods on both sides, and when I picked them up, one retreated deep into its shell, and the other stuck its neck out as far as it could and opened its mouth, threatening me.

I put the turtles in my truck—each shell about the size of a quarter—and drove a mile down the road, where I'd find a path leading me deep into the woods to release the turtles safely into a branch of New Hope Creek. I knelt down at the side of the creek, placed them both in the water, and in an instant, in the blink of an eye, they both disappeared. One buried itself in the soft muddy creek bottom, the other dashed into the deepest darkest water. It was humbling to see in that moment nature's harmonic wisdom that no matter what the predator's strategy, one of them would have survived.

When you are making your way in the future of unknowns and find two attractive opportunities or interesting solutions that are promising but look incompatible, don't compromise until you've reconsidered the question you are asking or the strategy you are developing to see if you can state it in a way that both can be true. The question shouldn't be "What does a turtle do to safely evade a predator?" but "What behaviors should be present within the clutch of eggs so that enough baby turtles will evade predators?"

Servant leadership

Talk about radical naivete; I imagine a time when we can simply say "leader" and presume the prefix. As we are navigating unknowable unknowns, servant leadership—with its humility, generosity, and determination to help others grow—will continue to be a critical skill. We need leaders who prioritize helping folks grow adaptive, resilient teams; precisely the behaviors needed for the unknowable future. To prepare for the future, servant leadership builds an organization where all can thrive. Servant leaders help folks make their best even better.

When an organization sees a leader using their authority to serve, they grant them more authority.

I tell my students and clients that the only authority worth having is authority granted to you.

As an entrepreneur, being a servant leader was the way to attract the very best talent I could. One way I would dramatize my determination to serve when interviewing someone would be saying something like "My promise is, if you come to work with us,"—as I'm rolling up my sleeves—"I will roll up my sleeves to work for you, for your success, helping you learn, finding you new opportunities."

Climate control versus command and control

The traditional "command and control" leadership model of rigid hierarchies and top-down orders will be increasingly ineffective in the unknowable future. Instead, the unknowable future calls for "climate control" leaders who intentionally nurture organizational environments where folks flourish. A leader can't demand a specific outcome from the unpredictable complex systems we all inhabit; they must identify the factors they can control and those they can influence and manage them so that it's most likely that the outcome is achieved.

The unknowable future will likely present times when problems outpace solutions, and fostering a dynamic, creative climate, not issuing orders, is the best way to prepare for that.

You noted overlap between servant leadership and climate control leadership?

Get your creative subconscious working for you

When I pointed out how hard your brain is working, twenty-four seven, most of that work is happening in your subconscious. It's continuously processing all your sensory inputs—sight and sound, smell and touch—engaged in pattern recognition, processing emotions, and autonomic functions like breathing and your balance.

Whenever it's time for me to share the following numbers, I first double-check that it hasn't been refuted, and each time I find new sources affirming it, I smile, sit back, and say "Gosh."

For you see, neuroscientists have determined that in the time it takes your conscious mind to process fifty bits of information, your subconscious has processed fifty million bits of information; not every neuroscientist reports those numbers exactly, but they all find a similar order of magnitude. Your creative subconscious takes all those sensory inputs it's continually attending to, it mashes them up with your thoughts, it aligns and contrasts the new with previous experiences, leading your thinking in a new direction now and storing it for future relevance.

Again, Steve Jobs had a useful insight when he described creativity as simply connecting dots, so make sure you have lots of dots. Your subconscious is continually collecting dots; you want to intentionally bust the status quo to take radically different perspectives so you aren't simply collecting more of the same dots.

What I find awesome is that your creative subconscious works for you without you being aware; taking intentional steps will help you enjoy the full benefits of its power. For instance, when working on a creative project and I see that I need to go for a car ride or get to go for a woods walk, I spend a moment before I depart and write a couple of sentences about the project and its ideas. I use a pen or pencil to write them on paper, which imprints the ideas onto the page and into my subconscious. Then I collect my dog and maybe a notebook and try to forget all about the idea until I sit under a tree or I head west on I-40 listening to music that I turn off as soon as the ideas demand it.

One of the best places to benefit from the idea of priming your subconscious and then leaving it alone is brainstorming with a group—this is useful for the next topic of creative collaboration.

Consider the traditional way a brainstorming session takes place. The team leader shares the current situation, a sense of the opportunity and possible goals, and some understanding of resources needed and timelines to respect, and then the leader says, "Okay, team, whatcha got, let's hear those ideas," and the group generates ideas.

Try setting up the session in a different fashion: take the team through all the information and current understandings, then excuse them for twenty-four to forty-eight hours.

When they return, they will have more ideas, more original ideas, more useful ideas.

Why? Because calling on your subconscious immediately doesn't give it time to do what it will always do, and that's to never stop relating the new inputs to your previous ideas, experiences, and knowledge bases. When you give it twenty hours to do its thing, and even better, forty-eight hours, there's time for full processing benefits.

Creative collaboration

I am reminding you that each of these creatively entrepreneurial behaviors has always been important; they are important in the future that is present, and their importance grows in the unknowable future.

Work of any significance—resolving a community problem, creating a needed organization, building an innovative product, or saving the nation—requires folks to work together. As you contribute your creative and entrepreneurial talents, you'll want to intentionally bring a version of your servant leadership—in this case, it's likely your best situational intelligence, sensing when you should step up and when to step back or when it's time for a different energy.

During creative collaboration, being intentionally generous with others, listening appreciatively to the best of their ideas, serves the team. And keep the lessons learned from brainstorming front of mind to look for ways the team can benefit from idea incubation.

Open-endedness

One of the companies I helped launch and grow with three incredibly talented partners was the innovative marketing services company FGI. This was in the pre-digital days. When an art director was designing a new ad or brochure they couldn't go online and download a place holder image for their layout; instead, they would draw a loose pencil sketch to represent what the visual would portray.

I found it interesting that time and again I enjoyed the pencil sketch more than the final artwork. I never examined why—our artists were award-winning, so it wasn't that their final work was disappointing. It wasn't until I became a student of creativity that I realized the incomplete nature of the pencil sketch called upon my imagination to complete it, allowing me to see it in a way that engaged me the most.

The open-ended images got me leaning in, involved. The final image caused me to stand outside and observe.

I apply this understanding to the collaborative work I do, offering incomplete starting places that, I hope, invite others to participate in completing them. As suggested throughout the book, the ideas here are presented less than fully formed, offered as pencil sketches for you to complete. I look forward to seeing where you take them.

RESOURCES AND EXERCISES

CREATIVE GREEN

Researchers from the University of Munich (UM) wanted to find out if color has an impact on creative performance. They were quite ambitious with their research design; most creativity researchers test one creative behavior, divergent thinking, but UM designed four creative exercises, each solved using a different creative approach.

After the control group completed the exercises, establishing a baseline score, the research participants were divided into five groups. Each group stared for thirty seconds at the color the researchers chose for that group before they completed the exercises. UM researchers tested red, blue, yellow, gray, and green.

Green was the only color that had an impact, and what an impact it had. Those who stared at green for thirty seconds had a 25 percent improvement in their performance versus the control group. Those who stared at the other colors had no performance improvement compared to the control group.

The researchers didn't speculate why only green had that

impact, but take a moment and look out your window wherever you are to see that the color of growth is green. The foundational process of life on this planet, the process that enables life, photosynthesis, takes in red and blue light and reflects back green. Our eyes detect more shades of green than any other color.

So twice a day, for thirty seconds each time, I stare at green not only for the boost but as a reminder of how important creativity is in our lives.

KICK THE STATUS QUO IN THE BUTT WITH A 30-DAY CAP

The status quo is the greatest impediment to creativity. As I mentioned earlier, I had long assumed the status quo I was trying to overcome was "out there," in traditions and bureaucracies, large institutions and organizations, and that's true but incomplete. The most challenging status quo hurdles are our brains.

Reviewing and adding to what was shared in the creative subconscious section above, our brains are working hard twenty-four seven—the brain is 2 percent of our body weight and consumes 20 percent of our energy—and it needs a break. The way it takes that break is by sending what you see or hear or think about down the same neural pathways it has been using, and your brain will continue that practice unless you interfere.

I invite you to have fun with your intentional interference and take on a 30-Day Creative Action Program, or 30-Day CAP. It's a simple idea. Every day for thirty consecutive days, you either:

A. Do something you've never done before, or
B. Do something you do frequently, but now do it in an opposite, contrary, radically different fashion.

For instance:

A. I have never stepped outside and given the first object I see a new name.
B. I brush my teeth right-handed. Today I will brush them left-handed.

With a bit of thought, as these examples show, accomplishing a 30-Day CAP can be integrated into your daily routine, so it doesn't take extra time.

Research indicates that completing a 30-Day CAP can improve your divergent thinking—the ability to identify lots of solutions for a problem, lots of options for an opportunity—by nearly 80 percent, and your convergent thinking—taking the best pieces from your ideas and shaping them into something new—by 20 percent. What you're doing is kicking the status quo in the butt just a little bit every day, and soon you'll have loosened its shackles so that new ideas and perspectives emerge.

More examples: I have never stood in line at a coffee shop, turned, and introduced myself to the person behind me. That's column A. Tonight I will sleep with my head at the foot of the bed. That's column B.

A tip: Planning the first three or four days of activities seems to serve many. Then, being more spontaneous as the 30-Day CAP continues, even bringing in some whimsy, is fun for most.

More examples: Some folks declare a digital sabbath,

column A. Some folks eat supper for breakfast and breakfast for supper for a day, column B.

To be clear: The new behavior of the day is for that day only and need not be repeated as part of the 30-Day CAP: Each day is a new activity. And don't be overly bothered if you aren't sure in which category a behavior fits—is eating dinner off a plate while standing up column A or B? You know when it's different from your usual, that's all that matters. And go ahead and use any of these examples—it's doing them that matters.

KEEPING A CREATIVE JOURNAL

Keeping a journal is a simple discipline to commit to regular use. Try seeing your journal as a fun opportunity to "let your freak flag fly" and cut loose with creative riffs and entrepreneurial rambles. It is important to stop editing yourself when developing creative ideas, and it is often most effective, again, when it is fun.

Just one way your journal entries pay off: It takes a certain understanding of a new idea or interesting thought to hold it in your head, to think about it. It takes a different sort of understanding of that idea to write it down. And it takes a new understanding of that idea to visually represent it. You are surrounding the idea, getting used to it, exploring its patterns.

Think about it. Write it down. Visualize it. Each step reveals something new.

If you hesitate at being visual in your journal because you tell yourself, "I can't draw," Bill Fick, a part-time Duke prof and full-time graphic artist and cartoonist, said to my students, "Trust the intelligence in your hand. Bring the pencil to the paper and set aside your judgment and just see what happens." Make that a colored pencil and see how that influences your expressions.

As you play with your ideas from all their angles, soon you are doing it naturally, as part of your intentionally creative mindset. Especially if you are having fun.

Do you want a journal that's compact and easy to carry, that's always with you? Do you want a large-format journal, so you can mark boldly at your desk at the end of the day? In any case, avoid lined pages.

Ideas for journal entries that accelerate your creative and entrepreneurial development:

- Going through your day, watch for examples of creative and entrepreneurial behaviors that generate something that wasn't there. What happens when folks, for instance, are playful with each other in their response to a situation? When you see it, wonder, then write a quick riff about it.
- Be mindful of good and bad design. When a product feels just right, or clunky wrong, think about why that is, then write it down or visually represent your experience with it. Services are designed, too, so when a store is not handling customers effectively or efficiently, think about the improvement that could be made and make it a journal entry.
- When you hear about a great business strategy, storyline, or innovative idea, don't just admire it, learn from it. Write or map why it's a great idea.
- When you come across a quote that resonates with your creative life or entrepreneurial experiences, write it down in your journal.

- Listen for interesting language, and wonder what it was that caught your attention when it does. Similes and metaphors are fun to listen for— they help us understand A by declaring its relationship to B, a useful, creatively entrepreneurial talent.
- Start a regular unknowable future series of entries to ruminate on what you've seen emerging.

Can you commit to two or three journal entries a week? If you are determined to not just grow your creatively entrepreneurial qualities but reclaim your creative genius, start journaling as you begin a 30 Day CAP. They will reinforce each other, accelerating and deepening your growth.

WALK

A 2014 study out of Stanford found that walking integrates the brain's hemispheres, the best state for your brain's creative work. Participants generated 60 percent more novel ideas while walking as opposed to sitting. Walking synchronizes the idea generation parts of the brain with the executive function of focus.

SIX-WORD CREATIVE AUTOBIOGRAPHY

Limiting ourselves is often a creative stimulant. Try writing your creative autobiography in just six words. Don't simply make a list of six creative attributes that describe you, but try to craft a narrative. In six words, you can't share your full creative life: just take a slice. Write it in your journal so you can look back at it later. Perhaps you'll want to compose another, then another.

My most recent: "Still looking for mountains to climb."

Another, submitted by a student: "Seams frayed, so I made wings."

SIX CREATIVELY ENTREPRENEURIAL TYPES

A few years ago, when IBM committed to nurturing the creative qualities of its employees, it developed a four-part taxonomy of creative types. The idea was to help their employees think about their individual creative and entrepreneurial motivations; the self-reflection would be useful at the beginning of their personal development program.

IBM asks its employees, "Are you motivated to be creative and entrepreneurial because you are . . ."

An Explorer? Are you excited by the unknown because you love discovering new ideas or opportunities?

An Artist? Do you need to express your personal vision, a vision for entertaining, informing, or serving others?

A Warrior? Do you love to compete, eager to use your creatively entrepreneurial skills to win?

A Saint? Do you love serving, want to help others, and want to use your creatively entrepreneurial talents to help make the world a better place?

Listening over the years to how folks applied these types to their own creative predispositions and behaviors, two more emerged:

An Orchestrator? Do you enjoy recruiting the right people and collecting the best resources for them as you help them identify their best opportunity?

A Cultivator? Do you enjoy taking on something someone else has started so you can use your entrepreneurial and creative abilities to make it even better?

I've offered this tool for personal insight to over five

thousand folks and have yet to find anyone who claims to be only one of these types; often, they are three or four. What about you? What's your combo?

After folks consider their motivations and identify their collection of types, I urge them to reexamine whether one of the creative types they didn't include might serve their continued growth or their work on an upcoming project or their preparation for an unknowable future, and how they might begin to incorporate those new qualities into their makeup.

You will enjoy even more insight—and have some fun—when you visually represent your combination. Graph it, map it, chart it, yes, for sure, but doodle it. Create a cartoon character. Find an interesting theme or visual style and have fun.

And invite family members or friends or colleagues to discover their types and share thoughts about why.

PROMPTS FOR "BEING CREATIVELY ENTREPRENEURIAL"

I don't define what it means to be "creative" nor "creatively entrepreneurial." Johann Wolfgang von Goethe (1749–1832) said, "Thinking is better than knowing," and while there are instances when "knowing" is paramount for sure, actively thinking about what it means for you to be creative and entrepreneurial is much more valuable to you than someone defining it for you.

Charles Mingus (1922–1979) said, "You can't improvise on nothing, man, you gotta improvise on something," so I offer a collection of behaviors and indications, facets and aspects of what being creatively entrepreneurial looks like, so you can craft your own understanding, the one most useful to you for your always-changing circumstances.

Being creatively entrepreneurial is intentionally:

- Seeing problems as opportunities to make things better by making better things, designing better services, developing better organizations, and forging better relationships.
- Looking at what others have been looking at and seeing what no one else has seen, which means intentionally stepping away from status quo perspectives or thinking, determined to break the bonds of the familiar.
- Being generative in the increment by generously delivering more in the inches and the minutes of daily life.
- Being ingenious . . . doing what you can with what you have where you are.
- Being humble . . . asking questions and retaining curiosity.
- Giving your undivided attention.

Designing . . . Adapting . . . Developing . . . Building . . . Initiating . . . Imagining . . . Discovering . . . Engineering . . . Narrating . . . Orchestrating . . . Growing . . . Nurturing . . . Inventing . . . Combining . . . Extending . . . Collaborating . . . Failing . . . Teaching . . . Learning . . . Appreciating . . . Refreshing . . . Painting . . . Leveraging . . . Experimenting . . . Providing . . . Storytelling . . . Fostering . . . Synthesizing . . . Cultivating . . . Pollinating . . . Exploring . . . Serving . . . Conversing . . . Leading . . . Risking . . . Empathizing . . . Aspiring . . . Playing . . . Failing again . . . Organizing . . . Celebrating . . . Thinking . . . Wondering . . . Wandering . . . Singing . . . Shaping . . . Constructing . . . Inquiring . . . Restoring . . . Caring . . .

Composing . . . Adjusting . . . Drawing . . . Trying . . . Attempting . . . Sustaining . . . Writing . . . Energizing . . . Investing . . . Researching . . . Fertilizing . . . Investigating . . . Helping . . . Questioning . . . Dancing . . . Trusting . . . Inviting . . . Renewing . . . Painting . . . Forging . . . Debating . . . Planting . . . Sharing . . . Providing . . . Sketching . . . Listening

Can you appreciate someone's new idea so it appreciates in value?

ACTIVITIES FOR CHILDREN

The focus here is on kids in the six-to-ten age range. Evidence shows that the wonderful creative genius 98 percent display at age four begins to recede just a few years later. Let's stop that from happening. Facing an unknowable future, they need to retain and grow their creative qualities.

The best approach to engaging children in this age range is 90 percent offering an open canvas and 10 percent an informed, playful invitation. With that in mind, you can create hundreds of variations on this simple structure for indoor open-ended play when you set aside a box, fill it with various odds and ends, and then:

- Ask the children to make the weirdest thing they can from those items.
- Challenge them to create a game using the items.
- Invite them to build a story using the items.
- Keep changing the items in the box to refresh play. A similar direction that doesn't need actual pieces is to announce their favorite playground is being threatened by the Evil Bulldozer, and they have a

rope, a bag of apples, a drum, and a ladder to use to save it. And next week, develop a new scenario.

And yes, for sure, use your best climate control strategies to minimize screen time. I feel a bit sheepish when I say that: My wife and I raised our three daughters before screens took over, so we never had to struggle with this challenge like so many of you do. Good luck.

A BIT ABOUT MY POLITICS

Does this quick political history support my nonpartisan claim? As I brought it together, I loved that my path reminded me of how Windy, my English Pointer, would cover a field when we were together hunting pheasants, racing forth, tracking back, always alert for a more promising scent.

At Southwood Junior High in Country Club Hills, Illinois—no hills, no country clubs—I was called a communist by my classmates in sixth-grade social studies class with Mr. Kahananui. That would have been 1962.

Mr. Kahananui was a most extraordinary man—proudly Samoan, which was more than a little mysterious to us. And he was determined to teach us the importance of something we'd never heard of before, the Third World, making sure we learned the role it was beginning to play in world politics. Before school started, my friends would take turns peeking through a crack in the gym door to watch him lifting weights and the next morning performing martial arts routines. He was also our gym teacher and taught us martial arts foundations, like how to fall and quickly roll back standing, prepared.

He was a man I wanted to impress, so with no more memory of my motivation than that, one night after a class on the US Constitution, I decided to make up a country so I could write its constitution.

I recall focusing first on the country's geography, then writing a history of its formation, then imagining the characteristics of the sort of folk culture shaped by place and founding. With the country realized, I began writing its constitution.

After a couple of nights working on it, I gave Mr. Kahananui the map of the nation, a summary of its history and culture, and its constitution. The next day, he called me to the front of the room and told me to read the constitution to the class. I don't recall anything I wrote but do remember that when I finished, two or three voices called out, "That's communism. Carl's a communist."

In high school, I was an athlete wanting to look strong, tough, and I romanticized joining the Army to become a Green Beret. I can still sing the 1966 "Ballad of the Green Berets."

Then, in the fall of my senior year of high school, I watched the 1968 Democratic National Convention on TV in our little house's tiny den. I had been sitting on the couch next to my father, but when he started cheering the Chicago police beating the protesters and the violence seemed to be spilling out of the TV and onto the floor, I slid down off the couch to join the protesters.

The next day, at preseason football practice, I walked into a locker room of teammates excited about going into the city that evening to beat on some hippies, though I don't think anyone did.

I had been working in Ontario as a fishing guide for a couple of summers by then, and I see now I was drifting left. Hearing successful businessmen sitting in my boat laugh their racial prejudices—offering to trade "their Blacks" for "your Indians" since they still knew their place was a common frame; I've cleaned up their language.

I shared a cabin one season with the camp store manager; a shelf in our cabin was filled with his books about Vietnam and the war and Western imperialism crushing Third World people. He was an American, from Colorado, a recent college grad; I never asked, but later concluded he was avoiding military service, perhaps dodging the draft, maybe AWOL. He shared the history of Vietnam since colonial times and explained what was happening presently in the country. I didn't know Ho Chi Minh approached the US delegation at the 1919 Paris Peace Conference hoping to gain our support in achieving independence from France, motivated by his admiration for the Founding Fathers. Nor did I know he and his militia worked with the US Office of Strategic Services during WW2, collecting information on the Japanese, reporting on troop movements.

By the end of the summer, any lingering notions I had of serving in the military had been laid to rest.

I arrived at Knox College in 1969, just as this small conservative liberal arts college in a farm town in Western Illinois did a deep dive into counterculture anti-war civil rights sex drugs and rock and roll—*Time* magazine wrote an article about the counterculture's growing impact at colleges across the country and noted Knox College's embrace as evidence it must be widespread and deep if it was even happening at Knox.

My fishing guide beard became a counterculture beard, and I dove in as well.

For reasons I can't recall, after college I started reading classic conservative political philosophy. My best guess is that years before I slid off that couch to join the protesters, through much of the sixties, I sat there fascinated when William Buckley and *Firing Line* was on our local public television station.

With extraordinary guests like Jimmy Carter and Margaret Thatcher, Muhammad Ali and Timothy Leary, Huey Newton and Groucho Marx, Noam Chomsky and Milton Friedman, Norman Mailer and Kurt Vonnegut, it seemed Buckley always had the most interesting things to say and said them in the most exciting fashion. He respected his guests' ideas even when he didn't agree; I sensed there was an authentic exploration of important ideas happening each Sunday afternoon, even if I didn't understand all of it.

Buckley must have led me to Malcolm Muggeridge and Russell Kirk, who led me to Edmund Burke, Thomas Carlyle, and Michael Oakeshott. As I explored their ideas, I understood I was, and I am, a populist by nature. The most beautiful piece of political poetry—of the people, for the people, by the people—is populist. The conservative view I was reading was one where progress and growth were the result of bottom-up self-organizing trial and error, a populist understanding of the healthiest, most sustainable growth, versus a liberal approach of distant views and uniform solutions attempting to direct and fix from the top down.

Buckley's first book, *God and Man at Yale*, was published by Regnery Publishing. A few years later, I was able to convince Henry Regnery Jr. to hire me just as he was assuming leadership of the company his father founded. Though Buckley had moved on to bigger publishing houses, they were close friends still, and the first time I was sent to NYC on business, Henry Sr. arranged for me to have lunch with Buckley and his senior editor at *National Review*, Joseph Sobran. During the lunch, after hearing a bit about my journey from counterculture fishing guide to conservative populist, they urged me to write a book about that journey.

Asides: Buckley shared with the table that he'd been so interested in trying cannabis that he sailed into international waters so he wouldn't break any laws when he took a puff—I was too shy to ask, and he didn't say if it was worth the trip. And at some point, his critique of liberals quotes them saying, "If I had some ham I'd make you a ham sandwich if I had some bread."

A constant background to my political worldview was my own version of Lost Cause Southern partisanship. I looked our evil sin in the eye and knew we weren't close to racial equity but could still romanticize the Fugitive poets and the Agrarian authors and their populist, anti-industrialist ways. I was a William Alexander Percy enthusiast; he lived across the street from my great-grandmother in Greenville, Mississippi, where I was born.

This silliness of mine faded away by my mid-thirties.

After 9/11, I was disappointed in the way our political leaders were talking to us. They were insistent that citizens had no role in this war on terror, a war they were waging on our behalf, asking us to carry on shopping like nothing was happening. When I thought about how proud my dad was when he told me about growing up during World War II, how citizens were enthusiastically supporting the war effort, collecting scrap metal and planting victory gardens and leading victory bonds sales drives. That made sense, that leaders would provide purpose for citizens that unifies us during wartime, during any difficult time for the nation.

I had a friend in the NC Republican Party who introduced me to then North Carolina Senator Elizabeth Dole's chief of staff. After hearing my thoughts and story ideas for leadership, he introduced me to mid-level employees of the just-established Department of Homeland Security; it was so early in their formation that the folks I met with the first time didn't have offices and used their old business cards. I was asked back to DC twice to share my presentation.

The presentation was the "First Defenders Education Program." It offered simple, useful ways citizens could help. For instance, do you recall that immediately after 9/11, airports instituted a 100 percent stop-and-search policy for every car before it entered an airport? To help the police carrying out the search, the program advised that before you leave home for the airport, you remove everything from the car, all the boxes and bags and blankets, and that as you approach the checkpoint with just your luggage, roll down all windows and pop open the trunk.

As the name of the program indicates, we recommended the title "first responders" be replaced with "first defenders." The logic was, folks would feel better when they sensed they were being defended from another attack, not only that we'd respond after an attack. It included the same professionals who heroically responded that day and then day after day—firefighters and state and local police—and added the Coast Guard, the National Guard, airport security, and others.

While there seemed to be appreciation for much of what was in the program—they did invite me back to share it with other staff—I have no evidence that it had any lasting impact beyond the two phone calls six months later from DHS employees I hadn't previously met, asking a series of questions, who reported that folks still referred to the booklet I created.

And after a false start sharing the ideas that led to this book, it was 2022 that I took this on as part of my calling, determined to do what I can to impact our political conversations—the level of interest early iterations received from Republicans and Democrats, Libertarians and Independents, and a couple of third-party representatives, motivated me to write this book.

This is the best place for the note about Buckminster Fuller.

He was a creator of human wisdoms and of engineering innovations. He was a provocative radical. His influence is felt in a number of professions. I was a fan, enamored by those ideas of his that I could grasp, however incompletely. As I was beginning to write this book, I learned, through the publication of a new book, that I couldn't admire the man. I still value his ideas.

THE 3 BOOKS I WAS READING WHILE WRITING

THE DAWN OF EVERYTHING

by David Graeber and David Wengrow

IT'S BEEN A LONG TIME SINCE A BOOK HAD AS LARGE an impact on my understanding of how life was lived and can be lived; it informed a new understanding of how we got here, and, thank you very much, it strengthened my optimism. For thousands of years, all around the world, our strategies for living together effectively—productively, freely, safely—displayed a political imagination I am calling on us all here to reclaim.

When I started reading it, I was in the first days of trying to understand the common ground discovery at the core of this book, and I continued to read it as the book became.

OURS WAS THE SHINING FUTURE

by David Leonhardt

I read *The Dawn* slowly; I read this one fiercely. It's another exploration of evidence from our past that shows we know how to organize more productively, more equitably, than we are today. In this case, the past is the second half of the twentieth century, or most of it. It's when capitalism envisioning prosperity for most had not yet been taken over by capitalism that enriches the very few; the more equity-based capitalist iteration was able to work with unions and government, and the nation flourished.

ABUNDANCE

by Ezra Klein and Derek Thompson

As soon as I heard of *Abundance,* I purchased and read it as I was rounding the turn and heading into the homestretch of writing this book. It offers a radically different lens to view scarcity and abundance. The authors focus on key policy areas like housing and reveal how well-intended progressive policies meant to protect environments and improve equitable outcomes may or may not have achieved their goals, but it is demonstrable that these policies created housing shortages and, therefore, larger unhoused populations. Cities with conservative leadership are permitting many more housing starts and have radically fewer unhoused.

Their message is solid: We need to get good again at making things we'll need, facing an unknowable future, creating a sustainable abundance.

CALLING ALL IMAGINAL CELLS

THANKS FOR READING. I KNOW I'VE TOSSED A LOT your way, but do you recall the very first was the suggestion you'd find love on every page? Was I close? Gosh, I hope so.

The chaos we face is not an opponent; it's raw material. You carry your piece of the code to transform the chaos through the daily work, stitching new nourishing flourishing patterns for our lives by starting the conversations needed now, supporting projects that reward generosity, casting your votes, and sharing your views with creative courage.

We'll create a future of sustainable abundance when we roll up our sleeves and get to work. And what might that work look like?

1. FIND FELLOW IMAGINAL CELLS.

A Ready Fire Aim strategy is to find friends fast, so let's go find more imaginal cells. You'll find them everywhere: the coworkers who bridge divides; the neighbors who plant community gardens; the school teachers doing what they can with meager resources; in the local chapters of community service clubs.

And there are likely a number of imaginal cells in your social capital network. Meet over coffee, take a walk, and swap ideas. Cluster to find how you leverage each other for each other and for the rest of us.

2. MAKE ONE IRREFUTABLY BEAUTIFUL THING.

Write a poem. Start a business that organizes itself in a most humane fashion. Find a graceful way of showing strangers you love them.

3. INTENTIONALLY GROW YOUR CREATIVE QUALITIES.

Help others grow theirs. Exercise climate control influences you have with young folks to help them choose to be and become their most creative selves—that is an irrefutably beautiful thing when that happens.

4. NAME THE CHAOS AND CELEBRATE ITS DISSOLUTION.

Call out greed, power grabs, betrayals—not with rage but with creative calm. This clarity is the first act of renewal. And as facades and systems crumble, go party with your fellow cells. Toast the chaos. When you do, invite me.

And to those in power or seeking it, folks, the age of performance outrage is over. The future of unknowable unknowns needs leaders who create prototypes and build bridges, not shout out blame to shame. Your most potent tool isn't a sound bite or a tweet. It's the stories about a single mom's side hustle mirroring the grit of a small business owner; about how climate solutions create jobs.

It's stories making the unimaginable believable.

The old political playbook was written for a game that died, without knowing, long ago. The new one is written with the language of creative and entrepreneurial unity and action, achieving a sustainable abundance regardless of the unknowable future's challenges.

You stoked? Great. I am too.

ABOUT THE AUTHOR

When Carl Nordgren was nine he had three ambitions. To be a novelist, a fishing guide, and play shortstop for the Chicago Cubs. He's two for three.

He started guiding at fifteen, from 1966 to 1971, at a wilderness fishing camp on the English River in Northwestern Ontario and on the White River in the Ozarks. His guests frequently told him to avoid soul sucking 9 to 5 jobs; these men were bosses of companies so he believed them. In 1970 the camps in Ontario were closed because of mercury poisoning, stories told in his novels, *The 53rd Parallel* and *Worlds Between*; after graduating from Knox College he was a foundry man and factory worker before joining a start up publishing company.

The first time he had an idea that created a new job he was hooked on the creative power of entrepreneurship; he spent thirty years starting companies and helping others start theirs. He was a pioneer in the cellular industry and led two new venture incubators. He's proud he's helped create many hundreds of jobs since that first one.

Invited to teach entrepreneurship at Duke in 2002 his course morphed into one that helped students grow their creative capacities and develop their entrepreneurial instincts and behaviors. He taught there for forteen years.

For twenty-five years his calling has been helping us become our most creative selves; he's the author of *Becoming a Creative Genius (again)*, teaches, and hosts the weekly radio show, 'Exploring your Creative Genius'. His calling now includes helping our nation appreciate the potential of the common ground he's discovered, common ground proven attractive to the left and right. There we find the most rational and optimistic way to prepare for the future of unknowable unknowns: be the most creative and entrepreneurial people we can be.

This common ground is home to policy ideas and communications strategies for politicians and community leaders to help us accomplish that.

Connect with him online:

THANK YOU!

Thank you for reading! The team at Torchflame Books hopes you've enjoyed this book and might consider leaving a review on Amazon, Goodreads, BookBub, The Story Graph, or anywhere else you like to track your recent reads. Alternatively, you could post online or tell a friend about it. This helps our authors more than you may know.

- The Team at Torchflame Books

Follow Torchflame Books for news about our authors and upcoming new releases @TorchflameBooks.

Find your next great read at torchflamebooks.com.

www.ingramcontent.com/pod-product-compliance
Lightning Source LLC
LaVergne TN
LVHW051012080826
845145LV00009B/2583

* 9 7 8 1 6 1 1 5 3 6 2 8 7 *